W9-CFI-878

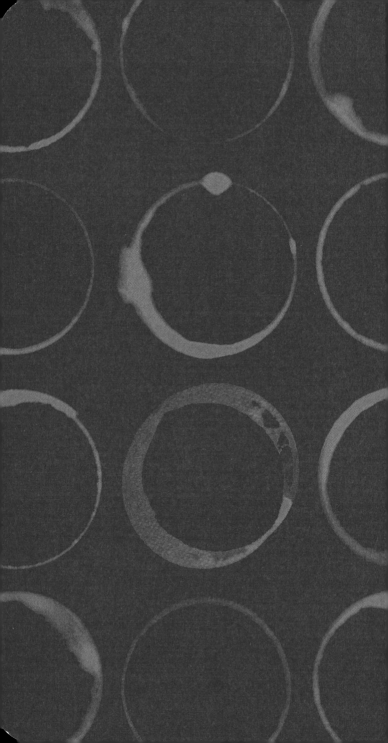

TOP 100 WINES UNDER $20

Had a Glass
2015

JAMES NEVISON

appetite
by RANDOM HOUSE

Copyright © 2014 James Nevison

All rights reserved. The use of any part of this publication, reproduced, transmitted in any
form or by any means electronic, mechanical, photocopying, recording or otherwise, or
stored in a retrieval system without the prior written consent of the publisher—or in the
case of photocopying or other reprographic copying, license from the Canadian
Copyright Licensing Agency—is an infringement of the copyright law.

Appetite by Random House® and colophon are
registered trademarks of Random House LLC.

Library and Archives of Canada Cataloguing in Publication is available upon request

ISBN: 978-0-449-01616-9
ebook ISBN: 978-0-449-01617-6

Printed and bound in the USA

Published in Canada by Appetite by Random House®,
a division of Random House of Canada Limited,
a Penguin Random House company

www.penguinrandomhouse.ca

10 9 8 7 6 5 4 3 2 1

appetite
by RANDOM HOUSE

Penguin
Random
House

CONTENTS

A Brief Guide to Wine Enjoyment

Had a Glass?

Welcome to Had a Glass. This is the guide for everyday wine enjoyment.

Had a Glass wades through the muck and murky liquid to point out 100 wines worth sipping. Consider it a vinous compass to keep you from getting lost in the wine aisles. Better yet, all the wines featured on these pages sell for under $20. Because wine is meant for everyday enjoyment, and every meal deserves a glass of wine.

Had a Glass is filled with the straight wine goods. Each wine is here for a reason, whether it is perfect for patio sipping, pairs remarkably with salmon, or simply inspires engagement in impromptu conversation. The wines come from all over the globe and represent a broad mix of grape varieties. There are reds and whites, not to mention rosés and sparkling, even a few fortified wines! It's true wine diversity, and true wine value.

Had a Glass is easy to use: pick a page, read the blurb, get the wine, and see what you think. Repeat.

> But remember: wine is best enjoyed in moderation.
> Know your limit and always have a safe way to get home.
> Such is the path to true wine appreciation.

Caveat Emptor and Carpe Diem!

Had a Glass goes out of the way to select wines that are widely available. Everyone deserves good wine, no matter what your postal code. While every effort is made to ensure prices and vintages are correct at publication, good wine buys sell out, and wines are subject to price variances and vintage changes.

It is recommended to use this book as a starting point for your wine adventures. Great bottles are out there, and as with all things worth searching for, the fun is in the hunt.

Wine, Barcoded

In a nod to interactivity, Had a Glass features barcodes for each wine. Given the proliferation of smartphones there are all sorts of uses for this handy addition. Using the growing number of available wine "apps," you can scan the barcodes to locate stores and availability for each wine. Or scan your favourite bottles to create your own personalized wine-tasting journal!

A Word about Value

"Value" is at best squishy and hard to pin down. Value is personal. And like scoring wine on a 100-point scale, it's tough for an objective framework to try to prop up subjective tastes. But whether you're after price rollbacks at a big-box store or hand-made designer goods, true value occurs when returns exceed expectations.

How is value applied in Had a Glass?

Most of the time the budget and bank account set a comfortable limit of my wine allotment at $20. On occasion I may spend more, but overall I toe the line. From research I know the majority of you feel the same. We all love great $18 bottles of wine. But we love cracking into a tasty $12 bottle even more!

Had a Glass celebrates wines that give you the best bottle for your buck: the $10 wine that seems like it should cost $15, the $15 bottle that stands out, and the $20 wine that knocks your socks off. Wine should be an everyday beverage, not a luxury—an enjoyable accessory to good living.

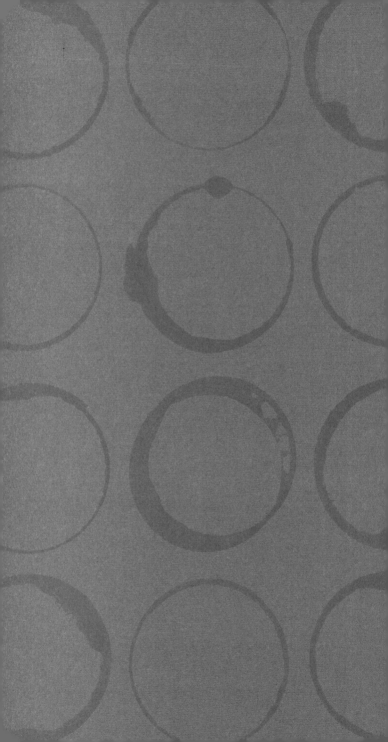

How to Taste Wine

Drinking wine and tasting wine are two different pastimes. Now, there's nothing wrong with simply wanting to open a bottle, pour a glass, and carry on. Indeed, most of the time this is standard protocol. Company has arrived and dinner is on the table and away we go!

But if you're ready to take your relationship with wine to the next level, it's time to commit to proper tasting technique. This permits a complete sensory evaluation of the wine in your glass, and I promise that it will add to your wine enjoyment as well.

You've likely heard the motto that a good wine is "a wine you like." Sure, at the end of the day taste is subjective and personal opinion matters. But what really makes a wine good? After you understand how to taste wine, you'll be equipped to make that call.

The Four Steps

There's no need to overcomplicate wine tasting. Nothing is more boring than listening to some wine blowhard drone on at length about the laundry list of aromas they detect, or slurp on for minutes as they attempt to pinpoint precise acidity and residual sugar levels. First impressions are often the best. Tasting wine is not a competition. It should be fun, which means yes, smile as you swirl and sip.

Here's the wine-tasting process in four simple steps:

Step 1: The look

You can learn a lot simply by looking at a wine. Tilt the wineglass away from you and observe its colour, ideally against a white background (a blank sheet of paper works in a pinch). White wines appear pallid straw to deep gold, and reds typically range from light ruby to the dark crimson of a royal's ceremonial robe—even at times the neon purple of grape Gatorade. A wine's colour can also hint at its age. Young white wines often have the brilliant sheen of white gold, a shine that mellows as the years pass and the wine darkens overall. On the other hand, red wines lighten as they age, superimposing amber and auburn tones on sombre claret. Also consider that while most wines are nearly transparent in the glass, an unfiltered wine may appear slightly cloudy with sediment.

Step 2: The swirl

To draw out a wine's aromas, give the glass a swirl. Use the base of a table for secure swirling, or raise your wineglass up high for an air swirl. Before you know it, you'll be swirling every glass in front of you, even if it holds water. The swirl not only helps release the aromas of a wine, it paints the sides of the glass with the wine's tears, or legs. These are the droplets that form around the wineglass and leisurely—or rapidly—make their way to the reservoir waiting at the bottom of the vessel. But note that while a wine's legs are fun to look at, they merely indicate texture and viscosity from residual sugars or alcohol, and don't necessarily suggest a wine's quality.

Step 3: The smell

Don't be afraid to put your nose right into the glass—wine tasting is not chemistry class and we need not adhere to a waft test. Smelling is wine intimacy, and a deep inhale will reveal what the wine is about. Many wine tasters feel the smell is the most important step in "tasting" wine, with scent seemingly hard-wired to our mind.

What are you smelling?

It's not me, it's the Cabernet! Many factors contribute to a wine's aromas, or smells. A wine can have myriad aromas of fruit (citrus, berries, melons, mango), which may at first seem odd considering wine is made from just grapes. Wine can smell of place too, be it sun-baked earth, rain-slaked slate, or even horsey barnyard. Of course, the winemaker and winemaking process can also influence a wine's aromas, from the smoke, vanilla, and spice imbued from oak to the yeasty brioche goodness imparted from barrel fermentation and sur lie aging.

It's also important to remember that smell is quite personal. Your apricot may be my peach. And I find the more wines you taste, the more comfortable you become addressing aromas. Further, it's not a contest to come up with as many olfactory adjectives as possible—though creativity can be applied in determining what's that smell. (See box on page 8 for examples.)

Step 4: The taste

Finally, take a generous sip of wine (it's fine to slurp as you sip, just as you would a mouthful of steaming ramen noodles!). Swirl it in your mouth. Swish it in your cheeks. Consider the wine's consistency and texture; this is what's referred to as a wine's body. Let your tongue taste the different elements of the wine: any sweetness from residual sugars, any tartness from acid, or any bitterness from alcohol. Tannins may dry your gums, making you pucker. Spitting is optional.

Wine Aromas

Commonly used words to describe wine aromas:	Unusual-sounding (but actually used) wine aromas:
citrus	cat pee
berry	wet stone
peach	burnt match
melon	rubber band
mango	cut grass
bell pepper	barnyard
flowers	baking bread
olive	diesel
nut	Tupperware
caramel	sweat
vanilla	cheese
oak	bacon
smoke	cracked black pepper
earth	tobacco
fig	tar

Understanding Body and Finish

Just like hair, wine has body. I find it easiest to think of a wine's body as its texture. And I still find the best analogy for understanding "body" is to think about milk. The consistency may be thin like skim milk (light-bodied) or it may be thick like cream (full-bodied). In the middle of the spectrum we have medium-bodied, the 2% milk of the wine world. Light-, medium-, and full-bodied are the three basic descriptions used, and it's perfectly acceptable to employ a range when describing a wine, say light- to medium-bodied for example.

However, all good things must come to an end, and a wine's finish refers to the lingering flavours and taste sensations that remain after it's been spit (or swallowed). The jargon is surprisingly simple to describe a wine's finish, which is generally described as short, medium, or long. That said, there's no simple formula for delineating each category. No point in getting out the stopwatch and clocking a wine's finish. In fact, there's no point in getting overly hung up on a wine's finish; better to move on to the next sip.

Wine-Tasting Tips

• Take notes! Whether you carry a leather-bound wine journal, scribble on a paper napkin, or tap away on a smartphone, take wine notes whenever you can. At the very least, jot down the winery name, grape variety, the year, and a thumbs-up or thumbs-down beside it. (No, you will not remember the wine the next day, other than perhaps that the bottle had a bird on the label.)

• When it comes to glasses, go big. And don't pour it more than half full. This will allow for proper swirling (as per Step 2).

• Practice makes perfect. Like you needed more motivation.

• But it's best not to practise alone. Tasting wine with a companion or group is a great way to gain multiple opinions and perspectives.

Suggested Wine Flights for Wine-Tasting Practice

Wine flights are a great way to practise tasting wine. The more wines you try, the better your frame of reference and the larger your internal wine database. A "flight" of wine lines up small pours of a few wines that share a common theme, allowing for great side-by-side comparison. It's like taking three pairs of jeans into the changing room!

Here are three wine flights for wine-tasting practice:

Flight 1: Tour de France

Without doubt, France is one of the most storied and important countries of the wine world. France literally has hundreds of different wine regions, all producing distinct wine. An entire lifetime could be spent just learning and tasting through the wines of France. As a starting point, this "Tour de France" flight takes you across three unique regions:

- Domaine La Rosière Jongieux Vin de Savoie (page 74)
- Bouchard Aîné & Fils Beaujolais (page 112)
- Château Pesquié Terrasses Ventoux (page 131)

Flight 2: Rosé around the world

It's great to see rosé wine finally rising in the ranks to fill more wineglasses. There's more pink wine in Had a Glass than ever before. Indeed, wineries around the world are producing more rosé, and while the rosé of Provence remains a pink wine benchmark, lots of global options now offer prime refreshment at principled prices. Here's a flight to get pretty into pink wine:

- Olivares Jumilla Rosado, Spain (page 84)
- Miguel Torres Las Mulas Cabernet Sauvignon Rosé, Chile (page 85)
- Quails' Gate Rosé, British Columbia (page 87)

Flight 3: Get indigenous

There are hundreds if not thousands of different grapes used to make wine. But most people can probably count the different types of wine they drink on both hands. Nothing wrong with this, but if you're looking to go beyond the tried and tested, line up this flight of wines made from lesser-known, indigenous grape varieties particular to a specific wine region:

- Plantaže Vranac, Montenegro (page 100)
- Monte del Frá Bardolino, Italy (page 121)
- Ramón Roqueta Vinya Nostra Xarel-lo, Spain (page 72)

It's the Wine's Fault

Unfortunately, there is likely a point in your wine-tasting career when you'll encounter a faulty wine. That said, with today's high-quality standards, in general there's less bad wine out there. Given our differing thresholds of perception, wine faults may be more or less apparent. But if you open a bottle and think something's funky, it might be due to one of these common wine faults:

- **"Corked" wine or cork taint.** Technically caused by a naturally occurring compound called 2,4,6-trichloroanisole (TCA) found in the oak bark used to produce corks, and attributed to improper cork sanitation. At worst, cork taint can leave a wine smelling and tasting mouldy like wet newspaper, but it can also mute flavours and aromas in general.
- **Oxidation.** Too much exposure to oxygen! A wine is particularly susceptible to oxidation after fermentation has completed and carbon dioxide levels have waned. Oxidized wine usually appears brownish in colour and smells stale.
- **Volatile acidity.** When fermentation goes awry, volatile acidity (VA) is usually the end result. VA shows itself in two main ways, through ethyl acetate, which smells like nail polish remover, or acetic acid—good ol' vinegar!
- **Too much SO_2.** The overwhelming majority of wines contain sulphur dioxide, which serves as a preservative and keeps wine stable. Some sulphur dioxide occurs naturally during the wine-making process, but most wineries also add sulphur dioxide. How much is a question of principle and philosophy, but if your wine smells like rotten eggs, it's faulty. If it has just a hint of sulphur dioxide, like a just-lit match, it may blow off and be fine.
- **Brettanomyces.** A funky, naturally occurring yeast behind such colourful wine descriptions as "Band-Aid" and "sweaty horse." Brettanomyces, or Brett, comes from the vineyard and can establish itself in the winery and winery equipment, especially if proper sanitation is not employed. But here's the rub: Brett gets personal. Some wine tasters like a little Brettanomyces in their wine and feel it adds character and complexity—but too much is funky gone off the railroad tracks.

How to Buy Wine

Buying a bottle of wine shouldn't raise heart rates or cause palms to sweat. Wine is fun, and strolling through your local bottle shop should be a joy. Wine-buying confidence has come a long way in the past decade, but there's no harm in offering a few tips to help your troll of the wine aisles.

Navigating the Wine Store

The typical liquor store or wine shop organizes its wine by country. This is helpful categorization if you're feeling geographic, but somewhat awkward if you want a Chardonnay and have to run around comparing one country's offering with another. Things can get particularly unruly if you head to a section with

French or Italian wines and are confronted with regional names emblazoned across the labels instead of the types of grape. No reason to panic (in fact, many traditional wine labels are starting to include the grapes along with the region). Get to know where certain grapes come from, and you'll be sleuthing through bottles in no time.

Where does wine come from?

Grapes are grown and wine is made in well over 100 countries. Entire books are written to cover the various wine regions of the world. This will not be another one. However, a quick primer can provide down-and-dirty generalizations to help you on your way to grape globetrotting.

Old World vs. New World

Before even delving into specific countries, it's important to discuss the Old World and New World of wine. Broadly speaking, the Old World refers to those countries around the Mediterranean basin that have thousands of years of grape-growing and wine-drinking history. We're talking France, Italy, Spain, Portugal, Germany, Austria, Hungary, Greece, et al. The rest of the globe's viticultural hotspots fall into the New World camp.

Traditionally, Old World wines have been typified as more austere and terroir, or place, driven. This is why the wines are usually labelled according to region rather than grape. New World wines tend to get labelled fruit-forward, ripe, and extroverted.

Of course, generalizations are handy but simplistic, and today the line between Old and New World has certainly blurred. You'll find French wines with cute marketing and grape names prominently displayed, and you'll find Chilean bottles touting adherence to Old World–style dry farming and wild yeast fermentation.

The key take-away? It's great to be a wine drinker in this Postmodern World, as the quality (and type) of wine widely available has never been better.

GrapeWHERE

So what happened to the Pinot Gris and Merlot on the label?
Don't fret if you don't see familiar grape names listed on the front of that
bottle from _____ {insert "Old World" country}.
Just remember this is where you'll find different grapes:

WHERE   Grape(s)

White wines

Bordeaux, France	Sémillon and Sauvignon Blanc
Burgundy, France	Chardonnay
Cava, Spain	Macabeo, Parellada, and Xarel-lo
Champagne, France	Chardonnay, Pinot Noir, and Pinot Meunier
Côtes du Rhône, France	Roussanne, Marsanne, and Viognier
Gavi, Italy	Cortese
Mosel, Germany	Riesling
Rioja, Spain	Viura (a.k.a. Macabeo)

Red wines

Barbaresco, Italy	Nebbiolo
Barolo, Italy	Nebbiolo
Beaujolais, France	Gamay
Bordeaux, France	Cabernet Sauvignon, Merlot, and Cabernet Franc (and maybe a little Malbec and Petit Verdot)
Burgundy, France	Pinot Noir
Cahors, France	Malbec
Chianti, Italy	Sangiovese
Côtes du Rhône, France	Mostly Syrah and Grenache, with Carignan, Mourvèdre, and Cinsault
Rioja, Spain	Tempranillo, Garnacha
Valpolicella, Italy	Corvina

Understanding Wine Labels

What's written on the wine label counts. You can learn a lot about a wine before you buy. The trick is to know what's worth reading. Wine label literacy can go a long way toward increasing wine enjoyment.

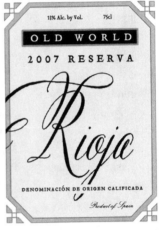

Wine or winery name

Back in the day, the name would be a château or domaine, or possibly it would be a proprietary name that was used by a winemaking co-operative. While these labels are still out there, brand names, animal species, and focus-grouped marketing buzzwords are now gracing wine bottles—all in an effort to help you remember what you drank.

Vintage

The year printed on the label is the year the grapes were grown. There are good years and bad years, typically determined by weather conditions.

The vintage is included for the wines reviewed in *Had a Glass*. Where no vintage is listed, the wine is "non-vintage," meaning it's been made from a mix of years. Non-vintage is quite common for sparkling and fortified wines.

Alcohol

Generally expressed as "alcohol by volume" (ABV), this tells you how much wine you can taste before the line between "tasting" and "drinking" becomes blurred. Or blurry. As a rough guide, higher alcohol content (14% is high, anything above 14.5% is really high) suggests a heftier, more intense wine. On the other side of the ABV spectrum, wines with less than 11% will often be off-dry (slightly sweet). High alcohol doesn't connote a better wine. It's all about balance, and regardless of the number, a wine shouldn't have the grating bitterness of alcohol—it's not supposed to taste like a whisky shot.

Grape variety

You pick up a can of soup and it's "mushroom" or "tomato." On a wine bottle you often see the grape variety: Malbec or Merlot or Chardonnay, to mention a few. These are your single varietal wines, as opposed to "blended" wines, which combine two or more grapes (such as Cabernet-Merlot and Sémillon–Sauvignon Blanc). Keep in mind that single varietal wines are no better than blends, and vice versa. Preference is dictated by your taste buds.

Appellation

Or, where the grapes came from. Old World wine often gives you the appellation instead of the grape variety. But appellations will also inform you about the grapes in the bottle. (See the chart on page 15.) Take an example from Spain. "Rioja," arguably the country's most famous appellation, describes where the grapes originated, and because Spanish appellation laws state only certain grapes are authorized in certain areas, the name also hints at what grapes made the wine. So, appellations (Burgundy, Chianti, Mosel) also help to define taste.

Appellations Around the World

When it comes to appellations, each country has its own terminology. Here are the common formal designations you'll see on wine labels, which indicate that the grapes used to produce the wine are from the demarcated region.

Country	Regional Designation
France	Appellation d'Origine Contrôlée (AOC or AC)
France	Vin de pays (VDP)
Germany	Prädikatswein (QmP)
Germany	Qualitätswein bestimmter Anbaugebiete (QbA)
Italy	Denominazione di Origine Controllata (DOC)
Italy	Denominazione di Origine Controllata e Garantita (DOCG)
Italy	Indicazione geografica tipica (IGT)
Spain	Denominación de Origen (DO)
Spain	Denominación de Origen Calificada (DOCa)
Portugal	Denominação de Origem Controlada (DOC)
Chile	Denominación de Origen (DO)
Australia	Geographical Indication (GI)
South Africa	Wine of Origin (WO)
United States	American Viticultural Area (AVA)
Canada	Designated Viticultural Area (DVA), regulated by the Vintners Quality Alliance (VQA)

Occasional Wine

Of course, regardless of how the wines are organized, we often buy a bottle for a certain occasion, be it to pair with Mom's meat loaf or to celebrate Sarah's birthday. This is a logical way to buy wine, especially—ahem—for the occasional wine drinker. But do you match the wine to the food or match the food to the wine? The answer will affect your wine-buying decision.

GrapeWHEN

Grape	WHEN
White wines	
Chardonnay	roast chicken, crab drizzled in butter
Chenin Blanc	pasta alfredo, satay
Gewürztraminer	curry, salad
Pinot Blanc	shrimp cocktail, minestrone
Pinot Gris	smoked salmon, brie
Riesling	rillette, turkey
Sauvignon Blanc	goat cheese, fried chicken
Sémillon	clams, pasta primavera
Torrontés	on its own, Peking duck
Viognier	halibut, ginger beef
Champagne	anytime!
Red wines	
Cabernet Franc	pork roast, vegetarian lasagna
Cabernet Sauvignon	porterhouse, kebabs
Carmenère	eggplant, grilled beef
Gamay	tacos, turkey
Malbec	venison, mixed grill
Merlot	Camembert, mushrooms
Pinotage	bison, goulash
Pinot Noir	salmon, duck
Sangiovese	lasagna, pizza
Shiraz	lamb, pecorino
Tempranillo	steak, bacon
Zinfandel	burgers, teriyaki
Port	in a cozy chair with a book

Feel the Wine

There's nothing wrong with getting emotional with wine, and another buying strategy is to match the wine to a mood. When staring at a wall of wine wondering what to put in the basket, consult your mood ring or do a quick self-emotive audit. Perhaps a bold evening calls for an aggressive wine, just as a mellow affair may require an equally subdued bottle? Looking for a little comfort? Head back to the tried-and-true.

Feeling	Try	From
adventurous	Riesling	Germany, B.C., or Australia
mellow	Pinot Noir	France or Oregon
assertive	Shiraz	Australia or Washington
apathetic	Chardonnay	anywhere
it's complicated	Cabernet blend	Chile or Argentina

Broadening Wine Horizons

While still on the topic of feelings, if you're feeling a bit adventurous, now is the perfect time to experiment with a never-before-tasted wine.

Like	Try	From
Malbec	Pinotage	South Africa
Cabernet Sauvignon	Tempranillo	Spain
Shiraz	Nero d'Avola	Italy
Chardonnay	Viognier	France
Sauvignon Blanc	Grüner Veltliner	Austria
Gewürztraminer	Ehrenfelser	B.C.

The Role of Vintages

Just when you think you're getting to know the nuances of a particular wine, along comes a new vintage! This is in fact one of the more exciting aspects of fermented grape juice. Wine is an agricultural product, subject to the annual vagaries of Mother Nature. If you want your wine to be the same year in and year out, you may as well buy Welch's. But how important is a wine's vintage?

A general rule is that it's easier to make good wine in a great year, but great grape-growers and winemakers can make good wine every year. A good vintage typically means great to ideal growing conditions: no untimely frosts, plenty of sun to encourage full and even ripening, and so on. That said, in a poor vintage, steps can be taken to minimize negative impacts.

So the vintage of a wine matters, but not to the point that it should limit your wine purchase. Indeed, for everyday wine drinking, vintages are usually not really considered. Now if you were investing in wine or looking to purchase bottles at an auction it would be a different story, but those aren't the types of wine you'll find in the pages of *Had a Glass*.

Corks vs. Screw Caps

There was a time, and we're still talking the 21st century, when a significant proportion of wine drinkers would rather drink water than be seen sipping from a bottle of screw-capped wine. Thankfully it hasn't taken long for most to realize that pulling a cork out of a bottle is only romantic until the first corked bottle, which seems to happen when there is no backup bottle at hand! And with an estimated 5% of wines with a cork subject to taint, this is a failure rate no other industry would rightfully tolerate.

So unless you're looking to cellar a wine for a particularly lengthy period of time, or you're risk-seeking and own an impressive collection of corkscrews, embrace the screw cap as an effective, efficient flavour saver. Anyways, it's not like corks are going to completely disappear anytime soon. Just don't be afraid to buy a wine based on its topper!

Returning Wine

If a wine is faulty, take it back! Generally this will be due to cork taint, though there is potential for other faults. (See page 11 for a review of common wine faults.) Just don't drink most of the bottle before bringing it back to the store! And no, it is not acceptable to return a wine simply because you do not like the way it tastes. Chalk it up to experience, take notes ruminating on your unmet expectations, and move on to the next bottle.

Avoid a Wine Rut

Becoming a little too comfortable with a certain bottle? It's great to have favourite go-to wines, but remember that it's a wide wine world. If your wining has been monotonous of late, consider these strategies on your next trip to the wine store.

Explore new wine frontiers

When you find yourself infatuated by a particular grape—be it cheerful Chenin Blanc or sumptuous Syrah—expand on your interest by seeking similar bottles from around the wine world.

Cabernet Sauvignon is a remarkably diverse grape, used both for robust standalone varietal wines as well as the backbone of notable red blends. Try travelling around the globe in the comfort of home with these three bottles: tour through the Cab Sauv of the Southern Hemisphere starting with the slightly smoky Nederburg Winemaster's Reserve from South Africa (page 99), then skip across to Western Australia for the rich and breezy Xanadu (page 128) before crossing the Andes into Argentina with a taste of Pascual Toso's approachable Cabernet Sauvignon (page 108).

Get a lay of the land

Certain parts of the world make certain types of wine. Cooler climate areas typically produce wines with higher levels of acidity, and conversely, warmer regions tend to produce riper grapes that manifest in rich, fruit-forward wines. This sense of place imbued in wine is one of the beverage's more enduring traits. Flipping through these pages, you'll see some great wine regions featured this year.

For example, take a closer look at Chile. The relatively narrow, Pacific Ocean–fronting and Andes Mountains–bordered nation offers a huge range of meso- and micro-climates, and grape growers are taking full advantage of this diversity. For 2015 a broad swath of Chile's wine regions are represented, from Lomas del Valle's Pinot Noir from coastal Casablanca Valley (page 115) to the classic vineyards of Maipo Valley by way of Undurraga's Sibaris Pinot Noir (page 117). Finally, head to one of Chile's newest (and coolest) wine region, the southern reaches of Bío-Bío Valley, care of Cono Sur's Single Vineyard Riesling (page 78).

Trade up

A winery commonly makes different tiers of wines, akin to a vinous version of Toyota versus Lexus. *Had a Glass* is all about the everyday sipper, but if you like what you're test-driving, look for the luxury version. For example, Mission Hill Family Estate is one of the largest and best known wineries in British Columbia. Their great value 5 Vineyards line of wines, such as the 5 Vineyards Chardonnay on page 61, will tackle meals Monday through Friday without breaking the bank. But just above the upper bound of *Had a Glass*'s imposed wine budget you'll find a number of Reserve-tier reds in the mid-$20 range. They also have limited release wines under the Select Lot Collection (~$35–$40) and Martin's Lane (~$26–$30) labels. And for a special occasion splurge, Mission Hill offers their top-drop white wine Perpetua (~$35), along with their Quatrain red blend (~$50), not to mention the peak of their Legacy Collection, the Bordeaux-inspired Oculus (~$70).

Alt Wine: Thinking Outside the Bottle

Now that the screw-cap debate has wound down, it's time to tackle a new frontier in wine packaging. Why are we so married to the wine bottle, anyways? After all, wine is made and mostly matured in either stainless steel tanks or oak barrels. Not to mention a heavy glass bottle is hardly the most efficient (nor environmental) means for storing wine in this day and age. Really, unless the motivation is about collecting wine and adding bottles to the cellar, there's no reason for bottle envy. Don't be surprised to see more alternative packages, from cask wines to wine on tap, arriving on shelves in the years to come.

Cask wine

Cask wine is nothing new, though it is certainly likely to be an increasing trend. Also known as bag-in-box wine—the more descriptive albeit less romantic name—these nearly indestructible vessels not only make great backcountry travel partners, they're also more environmentally friendly and create an airtight seal to help keep wine fresh longer once it is opened. Incorporating a plastic bag encased in a cardboard box, cask wine typically comes in three- or four-litre formats—though smaller 1.5-litre casks are starting to appear. Unfortunately, particularly in North America, cask wine carries the stigma of being high-bulk, low-quality produce, but around the world casks are used to contain some serious juice (and in reality, often cask wine is the same wine that goes into a producer's glass bottles). The fact remains, cask wine is a great package for enjoying wine.

Check out
Big House
Cardinal Zin Beastly Old Vines Zinfandel
$36.99 for 3L

It's three litres of wine (that's four standard-sized bottles) stuffed into an eight-sided box. Yes, this will make a statement on the dinner table, though for pure serving convenience it's likely better to keep this convenient cask wine in the kitchen and pour into a decanter for table side service. It's hard not to like this friendly red. Not only does it offer economies of scale to spare the pocketbook, it also provides ample ripe berry fruit, hints of toast and vanilla, and an über-smooth finish.

 Chili

 Ham and pineapple pizza

 Rock Out, Patio/Picnic

 United States

Aseptic Packaging, a.k.a. Tetra Paks

The issue with casks, of course, is that they still tend to be large volume packages. This is fine if the wine is intended for a restaurant or (very) large gathering, but three or four litres is a lot of wine, and even if the wine keeps for a longer period it's nice to have some variety (and food pairing versatility). Enter the Tetra Pak. This aseptic package pares things down to a manageable one-litre size while maintaining portability and a light weight. Heck, if it's good enough for all the fruit juice out there, it's good enough for everyday wine. Tetra Pak–packed wine has been available around the world for quite some time, although it's been slower coming to Canada. However, there are a few on offer on local shelves for sipping convenience.

Check out
Ciao
Sangiovese
$14.99 for 1L

It's organic, it's unbreakable, and it's (relatively) cheap! Sounds like a corny pitch, but it's true. And wait, there's more! Seriously though, the Ciao Organic Sangiovese is a great everyday wine option. It may take a bit of getting used to pouring from a Tetra Pak, but the reality is that this easygoing, black cherry fruit and violet-scented red holds it own against its value-minded, bottled Sangiovese brethren. Plus, it's camping-friendly, and guaranteed to taste great sipped at the top of the peak during your next backcountry adventure.

 Caponata

 Chicken Ballotine

 Wednesday Wine, BYO

 Italy

 Organically Grown

Wine on Tap

Wine on tap, essentially wine served on draught via stainless steel kegs, is being billed as the newest wine trend, but really it's only new to this part of the world. Throughout Europe, wine drinkers have long been able to pony up to the local wine depot or corner grocer with empty demijohn or Fanta bottle in tow for a quick fill. Granted, the kegs in question are usually huge plastic vats or oak barrels, and the wine on tap is typically everyday-drinking table wine.

The current push for wine on tap promotes both quality and locality, an approach that complements perspectives of sustainability quite nicely, particularly in western Canada. In British Columbia, given the proximity of Okanagan vineyards, it makes sense for many wineries to forego the bottling process in order to get wine to market as quick and conveniently as possible. So don't be surprised to soon see local Pinot Gris on tap next to the Pilsner and IPA!

Check out

While regulations don't (yet) allow consumers to head down to the liquor store with refillable wine bottle in hand, wine on tap is becoming readily available at a growing number of restaurants. And a visit to the Vancouver Urban Winery located in the city's downtown east side really showcases draught wine. Not only is the facility responsible for getting an increasing number of winery's wares out of cask and into keg, the "urban winery" features a tasting bar equipped with 36 wines on tap!

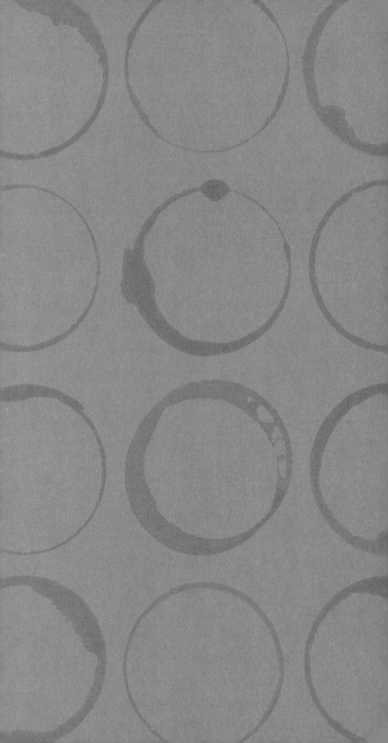

How to Enjoy Wine

Wine is like golf. There is a huge array of specialized accessories. But all you really need to play the game is a set of clubs and some balls. Likewise, all you really need to enjoy wine is a bottle and a glass. From there, it's up to you to decide how much you want to invest and how much shelf space you want to devote to storing wine paraphernalia.

Glasses and Stemware

Crystal? Stemless? Plastic tumbler? Mason jar? The wineglass options are varied, and while not all glasses are created equal, drinking wine from any glass can be equally enjoyable.

It's true that you can buy a different glass tailor-made to

each type of wine. While there is no harm in gathering a glass collection, it's definitely not a necessary pursuit to maximize your wine enjoyment. A set of good white and red glasses (Chardonnay- and Bordeaux-shaped make sense) will suffice, and a standardized ISO tasting glass is helpful to really take wine tasting seriously. But at the end of the day, when a wonderful meal is waiting on the table, a simple juice glass works as well!

Good stemware has its benefits

- Swirling wine in the larger bowl common to fancy glasses does wonders for releasing a wine's aromas. And it's best to pour a few fingers at a time to get a proper swirl going.

- Holding a glass by its stem helps keep white wines chilled, and it also keeps grubby fingerprints off the glass!

- A glass with a thin rim certainly provides an elegant tactile sensation.

Note: The stemless wineglasses that have recently become popular may get marked up with fingerprints, but they fit great in the dishwasher!

Decanters

After glasses, the next most important wine accessory is the decanter. It provides both form and function, and is a secret to getting the most out of your wine.

Decanters have typically been associated with old wines, and it is true that decanting old wines to remove the liquid from the sediment will keep your teeth clean. But how often do you find yourself drinking aged wine?

In these contemporary times, the best use of a decanter is as a wine time-machine! Use your decanter to decant young wines, allowing them to breathe. Most wines we buy are consumed young—often too young—and decanting will open these wines up, smoothing their fruit and revealing their true character. There's no magic formula for how long to decant a bottle before drinking, and don't be afraid to give the wine a vigorous shake, but as a general rule most red wines appreciate an hour in the decanter. Try "airing" lighter reds for half an hour. White wines don't really need to decant unless you just like the look of it.

Anything can be used as a decanter, from a clean teapot to a juice jug. To get serious about your decanter, find a glass or crystal container with a wide base and a narrow opening. This facilitates swirling, makes for easier pouring, and looks styling on the table!

Corkscrews

Butterfly

T-Bar

Waiter's Friend

Wars have been fought over broken corks. Well, perhaps not, but it certainly is disappointing when a cork is mangled and broken into bits at the hand(s) of a bad corkscrew. (Actually, wine—and the supply thereof—has certainly been a fixture in many wars over the years.)

A corkscrew does not have to be intricate or expensive: a good corkscrew simply needs a well-wound worm (the screw part that winds into the cork) and some decent mechanism for leverage. Avoid corkscrews with worms that resemble a drill bit or wood screw, as these culprits typically do more cork ripping than pulling. Past experience shows these latter worms are most often found on the so-called butterfly corkscrew.

Purists might opt for the good old-fashioned T-bar corkscrew, which certainly hints at nostalgia and can make quite the design statement when the worm is grafted to an old hunk of grapevine à la rustic French fashion. Just be ready for a firm forearm workout, and be prepared to shove the wine bottle between your legs (or feet) for stability and leverage. Gadgetphiles may be drawn to the fancy, pneumatically assisted, and gear-operated corkscrews available, which work just fine but tend to cost the equivalent of a couple good bottles.

For the best all-around corkscrew there's none better than the waiter's friend. Resembling a pocket knife, this simple corkscrew is the go-to option for servers and sommeliers the world over. It tirelessly opens wine bottles, and usually includes a small knife for cutting through bottle foils as well as an integrated crown cap opener. The waiter's friend is cheap (they're pretty easy to find at thrift stores for a couple bucks) and effective (never yet met a cork it couldn't beat), and makes you look like you mean wine business when looped around your belt.

Collecting Wine

Starting a wine collection is a fantastic way to expand your wine enjoyment. Sure, a fancy cellar with custom millwork, temperature control, and cobwebs-placed-just-so is a beautiful thing, but the 99% of us that don't have the space, the resources, or the patience for such a cellar needn't be deterred from collecting wine.

Start your wine collection simply with a bottle each of red, white, and sparkling wine. Keep the white and bubbly in the fridge and replenish as required. This vinous triumvirate ensures you're prepared for any impromptu occasion. Add to this base collection by picking up bottles while travelling, or perhaps track down a wine you had at a restaurant and really enjoyed. The key is to tie the wines to personal experience, which will add to enjoyment when you finally get around to opening a bottle. If the wine will be consumed in a year or two, simply keep it displayed in your wine rack or in the corner of a closet.

Of course it's important to keep wine storage in perspective. More than 90% of wine sold today is made for drinking now (or in a week, three weeks, six months). There is wine for aging and there is wine for drinking, and this book is about the latter. But there's no denying that wine evolves as it gets older, and a wine that is made to cellar can metamorphose into a completely different beverage, replete with aroma and flavour nuances not permitted in young wine. Just make sure to do some research if you plan on buying wine to enjoy in decades to come.

A Starter Cellar

Curious about aging wine? Just as raw denim takes time to meld and mould and come into its own, the maturing process can add real character to the right wine. Here is a mixed half-case culled from wines reviewed in this book. Put them in a box, place on its side, and shove away in the basement or seldom-used closet and see how they develop in three to five years.

1) Cono Sur Single Vineyard Riesling, Chile (page 78)
2) d'Arenberg The Hermit Crab Viognier Marsanne (page 79)
3) Amalaya Malbec Blend, Argentina (page 130)
4) Charles & Charles Cabernet Sauvignon Syrah, United States (page 124)
5) Crasto Douro, Portugal (page 132)
6) The Wolftrap Syrah Mourvèdre Viognier (page 110)

Wine-Serving Temperatures

red wine	18°C (65°F)	a bit below room temperature
white (and rosé wine)	10°C (50°F)	20 minutes out of the fridge
sparkling and sweet wine	5°C (40°F)	straight from the fridge

Tips
• The above chart provides general guidelines, but personal preference trumps suggestions.

- Lighter red wines (such as Gamay Noir and Valpolicella) are often enjoyable served a bit cooler, especially when the weather is warm. Conversely, richer white wines (such as Chardonnay) show more complexity served a little warmer than usual.

- Err on the side of serving a wine too cold. The bottle will always warm up as it sits on the table.

- If a wine is sweet, serving it cold will make it seem drier and more refreshing.

- All dessert wine should be served at fridge temperature, unless it's red—like port—in which case you should serve it at the same temperature as red wine.

The Dregs, or Leftover Wine

It's true that wine starts to deteriorate once the bottle is opened and the wine is exposed to oxygen. But how much time do you have before the bottle goes bad? Generally, polishing off a bottle the following day—or if you must, even the day after—is fine.

Yes, there are strategies to postponing a wine's demise. All manner of vacuum pumps and inert-gas sprays are available to attempt keeping O_2 at bay. If you're wary of accumulating any more wine gadgets, you can simply replace the cork or cap and place the bottle in the fridge—whether white, pink, or red—to slow down the oxidation.

If all this sounds like a lot of effort, you may simply be better off breaking out a chunk of cheese and pouring the dregs around!

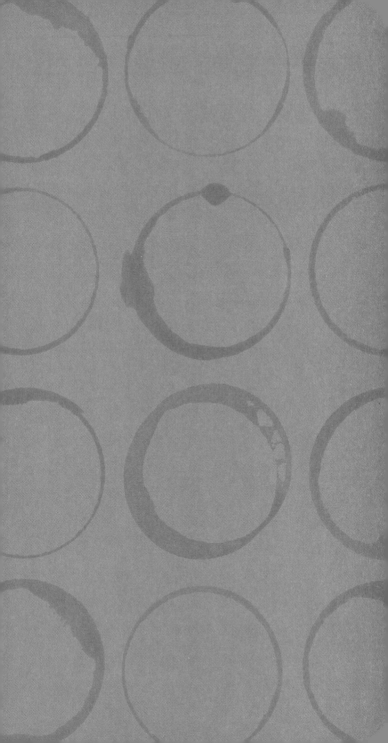

Food and Wine

Wine without food is like treble without bass. Sure they can exist separately, but the two really work together to create a whole. Of course, put notes together willy-nilly and there's no guarantee of musicality. Same with wine. The food and pairing strategies below serve to help you find harmony in order to turn up the gastronomical stereo!

Red meat

Serve red wine. "Red wine with red meat" is one adage that rings true. Beef, lamb, and game are hearty. They're full-flavoured and heavy. They're packed with protein. Red wines—especially Cabernet Sauvignon, Malbec, Merlot, and Syrah—follow the same traits. Plus, hearty red wines tend to contain more tannins than other wines, and protein works wonders in smoothing out tannic wine.

Poultry

Serve fruity medium-bodied white wine. Everyone likes chicken, right? And nothing beats a holiday-festooned turkey. Similarly, most people are happy with dry medium-bodied white wine. We're talking Pinot Gris, Sémillon, and friends. If you want to get creative, try sparkling wine.

Pork

Serve medium to rich whites, light to medium reds. The "other" white meat can take to a lot of different wines. An off-dry Riesling goes gangbusters with roast pork (don't forget the applesauce), or if your wine choice swings red, opt for a lighter rosso from Italy's Veneto region, or Gamay Noir in general. Ground pork stir-fried with an Asian twist is a prime partner for exotic, aromatic Torrontés. The bottom line is that pork is highly wine-friendly; it really depends on how you sauce the swine.

Fish

With delicate fish serve light to medium white wine. The way you cook the fish makes all the difference. The delicacy of a poached fish needs a delicate wine like Pinot Blanc or Soave. If you're baking, seek a bit more texture from a white Bordeaux blend or Pinot Grigio. Frying in a glorious sea of butter? Open a Chardonnay or a sparkling wine. Overall a good strategy to follow is: the oilier the fish, the heavier the wine can be.

With firm fish serve medium white or light to medium red wine. Any fish that can be sold in "steaks" qualifies in this camp. For example, wild B.C. salmon has plenty of flavour, and it takes a wine with extra heft to get along with it. Likewise, halibut is no shrimp. White-wise, try both oaked or unoaked Chardonnays and Viognier. Red-wise, try a Pinot Noir. And don't forget rosé.

Shellfish

Serve light white wine. Look to fresh, crisp wines—just how you want your shellfish to be! Consider how lemon or lime are often employed with seafood to perk things up, then consider wines with comparably high acidity. It's also safe to bet on white wines with no, or neutral, oak flavour. Albariño, Chenin Blanc, and Riesling are bivalve- and crustacean-friendly. Sparkling wine is another refreshing, go-to option.

Vegetarian

Serve wine similar in flavour and texture to the veg. No offence to soy protein, but what's up with tofurkey and meatless meat substitutes? Vegetarianism and veganism are noble pursuits in their own right and can be celebrated as such (with wine). Vegetables, grains, legumes—all pair with vino. Simply consider flavours and texture. Earthy, hearty dishes featuring mushroom or eggplant go great with heartier, earthy reds. Lemon-splashed quinoa salad fares well with citrusy Sauvignon Blanc.

Spicy

Serve fruity, off-dry, and lower-alcohol white wine. Wine and spice can make strange bedfellows. Keep the capsaicin in relative check, and a slightly sweet, fruity wine like Gewürztraminer or an aromatic white blend will show through the spice. But if the food is heavy on jalapeño, go with beer.

Dessert

Serve red or white wine that's sweeter than the dessert. If the wine is too dry, the sweet dessert will make it seem even drier. And blander. Look for fortified wines like port and Marsala that are sweet but not cloying, or a lively and spritzy Moscato d'Asti to keep things light.

Oh, and a word about chocolate: it's harder to pair the cacao than you think. Stick to quality dark chocolate and still heed the advice to stay sweet with the wine. Grenache and sparkling Shiraz make interesting options, or for a different approach, try a fruit wine and drizzle a corresponding fruit sauce over the chocolate!

Cheese

Try anything. It won't hurt. A wine salesperson once said, "If you want to sell wine, serve cheese." Cheese makes everything taste good. Cheese is highly recommended before dinner, during dinner, and definitely after dinner. Creamy cheese is tasty with a creamy wine like white Rhône blends, harder aged cheese sings with a solid wine like Carmenère. And a beautiful match that never goes out of style is salty blue cheese and sweet Sauternes or late-harvest wine.

Food and Wine Pairing Tips

- Consider intensity. Big-flavoured wines tend to go with big-flavoured foods. What does "big-flavoured" mean? Full-bodied, fruit-forward wines you really feel in your mouth. The corollary is that light-flavoured wines tend to suit lighter dishes (the wildcard is sparkling wine, which seems to be able to go with just about any food thanks to its overtones of refreshment and celebration). This is the key reason why a robust Malbec runs roughshod over mixed greens but is amazing with a mixed grill.

- Either contrast or match food and wine flavours. A buttery Chardonnay matches a creamy alfredo sauce, and a meaty Cabernet matches, well, meat. On the other hand, a crisp and fruity Sauvignon Blanc works wonders in contrasting briny, rich oysters—and a fizzy, slightly sweet Lambrusco can tame a plate of fully loaded nachos.

- It's OK to play with your food. Just opened a Shiraz with an extra peppery kick? Try grinding a bit of black pepper on the dish to bridge the gap. Is that zesty Albariño overpowering the seafood? Squeeze a few drops of lemon juice on your fish to help things jive.

- Build flavour bridges. Can any wine go with any food? That's a stretch, but if your food is balanced in flavour, you stack the odds in favour of a successful match. A steak or salmon on its own is a recipe for the doldrums, but a sprinkle of salt or a bit of lime will give the food some seasoned balance. A garden salad with a handful of roasted pine or pumpkin nuts (or bacon bits!) to flesh out an acidic vinaigrette will increase the wine-pairing potential.

• Keep things in perspective. Food and wine matches are moving targets. One night's perfect match may not prove as memorable the next day or week. Context and company also go with the wine and food.

Icon Maps

There is a wine for every meal, and there is a wine for every occasion. These icons will appear alongside each review to offer a few suggested food pairings and occasions to enjoy with every wine.

Food Icons

	Beef	Big protein, whether it's roast, steak, or stew
	Cheese	Hard or soft, stinky or mild
	Dessert	Sweet, sticky, fruity, and fun!
	Fish	Big or small, whole or fillet
	Lamb	The other red meat
	On its own	'Nuff said
	Pork	Chops, kebabs, loin—from nose to tail
	Poultry	Turkey, chicken, duck, and any fowl
	Shellfish	Bivalves and crustaceans
	Vegetarian	Garden-approved and tofu-friendly

Occasions

BYO　　　　　　Crowd-pleasers; wines to pack along
　　　　　　　　　to the dinner party

Classic　　　　　Wines that show good typicity;
　　　　　　　　　varietally true bottles

Patio/Picnic　　Sunshine in a bottle; sipping wines ready
　　　　　　　　　for alfresco dining

Rock Out　　　　Wines to let your hair down and crank it up to 11

Romance　　　　Wines to get busy with

Wednesday Wine　Everyday bottles to get you through the
　　　　　　　　　mid-week hump

Wine Geek　　　Eclectic wines outside the usual bottled domain

Winter Warmer　Wines to ward off any chill

 Look for this icon to occasionally appear on the neck of
wine bottles. It's an indication that the wine is made from
organically grown grapes.

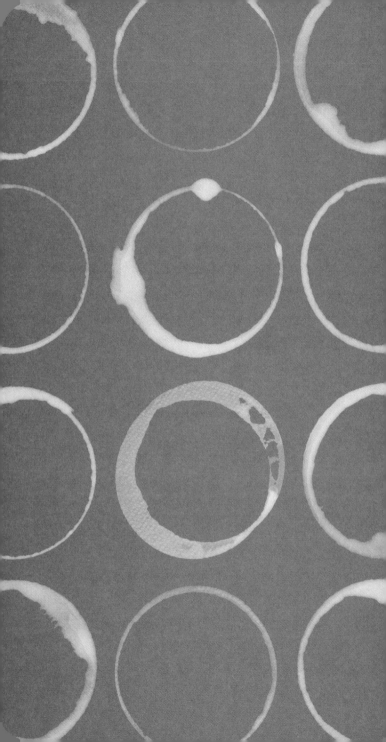

The Whites

South Africa

Obikwa

2013 Sauvignon Blanc
$9.99

This year's 10-dolla-brawla award goes to Obikwa Sauvignon Blanc! That's $10 brawler, as in the 10-buck bottle that isn't afraid to punch above its price class. Look, this white isn't going to win *summa cum laude* of Sauvignon Blanc, but it is certainly going to hit the mark on providing maximum enjoyment and minimum investment. Nice citrus, a slight herbaceousness. It has the hallmark modern-day Sauv Blanc qualities—right down to its gutsy mouthfeel and crisp finish. It's an easy quaffer, and easy on the pocketbook.

 On its own

 Grilled sesame ginger tofu

 Wednesday Wine, BYO

6001108004031

Cono Sur

2013 Bicicleta Viognier
$10.99

This is a perennial super-value pick. It's as simple as that. Cono Sur continues to overdeliver with their everyday-priced Bicicleta line of wines (it means bicycle in Spanish). The latest vintage of Viognier, which is made from grapes grown in the winery's extensive vineyards in the Colchagua Valley, is especially exuberant. Exceptionally aromatic with honey, peach, and flower blossom, it sports heady richness and a tickle of spice before ending with a fresh, balanced finish. Pair with grilled chicken, or sip solo on the back deck.

 On its own

 Grilled chicken

 Patio/Picnic, Winter Warmer

07804320405407

Dunavar

2012 Muscat Ottonel
$10.99

There's nothing shy about Muscat Ottonel. A member of the naturally exuberant and aromatic Muscat family of grapes, Muscat Ottonel is used to make both sumptuous sweet wines and dry whites. The latter is the tack Dunavar takes in its Muscat Ottonel, which offers a bang-up introduction to this gregarious grape at a bargain-basement price. Floral, citrus, and spice notes abound in this medium-bodied, fresh, but rich white that is certainly "best served well chilled," as per the label instructions. Pair with tamed-down chicken curry or even sip solo; it's like a light-therapy lamp for the taste buds.

 Tuna sandwich

Easy-on-the-spice
chicken curry

 Classic, Wine Geek

Gazela

Vinho Verde
$10.99

I'll be the first to admit it: this is one of those wine-lifestyle picks. I can't think of the last time I sipped on Gazela VV outside of summer, but you know, it really serves its thirst-quenching purpose. It's just lots of citrus and acidity in a slightly spritzy package that will save you the extra step of adding club soda to your favourite cheap white. Perfect for sipping neat to beat the heat, or feel free to add fresh sliced or muddled fruit for a fancy tipple.

 On its own

 Baked Brie puff pastry

 BYO, Patio/Picnic

5601012045505

Chile

Santa Rita

2013 120 Sauvignon Blanc
$10.99

A year ago, I found this wine bold and fruity with a tongue-lashing of freshness. Then the 120 hit all of Sauvignon Blanc's high notes at half the price of many other offerings. Well, this year it's half the price minus two dollars, which of course makes it an even better buy. It has the exuberant tropical fruit and herbaceous aromatics, the zesty and zippy mid-palate, the persistent perky finish, and the capital-F Fun we've come to expect from New World Sauvignon Blanc—traits that continue to put a smile on every diner's face.

Cod and chips

Vegetable tempura

Patio/Picnic, Classic

089419007091

Calona Vineyards

2012 Artist Series Sovereign Opal
$12.99

Every grape has a story.
Sovereign Opal's is a uniquely Canadian tale. The grape, an esoteric crossing of Maréchal Foch and Golden Muscat, was developed at the Pacific Agri-Food Research Centre in Summerland. Sovereign Opal was specifically bred to be hardy enough to sustain Okanagan Valley winters while maintaining good aromatics and fruit. And it is deliciously aromatic, with great floral notes and tropical fruit, offering significant character for the price. Ever so off-dry but balanced by freshness, it's a great everyday, food-friendly white.

 Guacamole and chips

 Panko-crusted snapper

 Wine Geek, Wednesday Wine

00058976260041

France

La Vieille Ferme

2013 Blanc
$12.99

Grab and go. For those evenings that call for a quick decision, when work has drawn on and there's no mood (nor time) for dilly-dallying, it's easy to count on La Vieille Ferme. It comes in all stripes—well, at least the white-pink-red colours of wine—and the latest vintage of Blanc is particularly boisterous. A blend of four grapes common to the southern Rhône (Bourboulenc, Grenache Blanc, Ugni Blanc, and Vermentino), it's both robust and vibrant, with nutty notes, stone fruit, and green citrus leading to a lingering fruit finish. Great intensity overall belies the light price point, making this a true midweek sipper.

 Chicken tenders

 Cutlets in mushroom sauce

 Wednesday Wine, Classic

631470000049

Italy

Masi

2013 Modello Bianco
$12.99

Great everyday white. Great everyday white. **Point made.**

 On its own

 Smoked salmon

 Wednesday Wine, Patio/Picnic

8002062001560

Italy

Ruffino

2013 Orvieto Classico
$12.99

Wines from Orvieto have been described as "the sun of Italy in a bottle." Unfortunately, I can't ascribe these words to anyone in particular, but they do nicely capture the essence of these cheery whites. Orvieto is in Umbria, next door to—but hordes away from—the tourist track of Tuscany. Same generous sun, same warm spirit. But here, white wines take the prominent bit of the spotlight, and for 13 bucks, this one should be highlighted atop your table as well. A blend of typical Umbrian grapes (Grechetto, Procanico, Verdello, and Canaiolo Blanco), it's full of citrus, floral, and apple notes with good texture and finesse on the finish.

 Fennel crostini

 Mozzarella

 Wednesday Wine, Classic

8001660126750

South Africa

The Wild Olive

2013 Old Vines Chenin Blanc
$12.99

The vineyards of South Africa have historically been awash in Chenin Blanc vines. It was initially planted in large part due to its propensity for generous growth—a boon for the local brandy industry, if not overall quality. The upside is a bevy of "old vines" Chenin Blanc that, when given attention and care, can produce some remarkable wines. New to our shelves, The Wild Olive coaxes fruit from 30ish-year-old vines for its straight-up CB. Early harvesting and full stainless-steel fermentation create a fresh, leaner-style Chenin, displaying characteristic waxy citrus and lanolin qualities and a round, candied-lemon finish.

 On its own

 Vietnamese salad rolls

Romance, BYO

6009900162614

France

Paul Mas

2013 Viognier
$13.99

They'll think you spent more.
It's one of the great things about
Paul Mas wines. Of course,
image isn't important. But you
know, sometimes it is. And
sometimes you want to have
enough money left over to buy a
baguette and a hunk of cheese.
From a superficial standpoint,
the Paul Mas bottle both looks
classy and feels solid (we're
talking paperweight territory) to
the touch. But it gets better.
Pour a glass and you're offered
great stone-fruit and floral
aromas in a subtly rich white
with added complexity and a
hint of wood spice thanks to
partial oak aging.

 Schnitzel

 Chèvre

 Wednesday Wine,
Winter Warmer

3760004420127

Argentina

Crios de Susana Balbo

2013 Torrontés
$14.99

Tasting this wine always makes me think about having my mouth washed out with soap. But in a wonderful way that's just for grown-ups. Impossibly floral, gushing rose petal and orange blossom, its engaging aromatics are offset by a rich, lush texture and smooth, fresh finish. This unoaked white would pair wonderfully with grilled chicken or fish, but it's also great for solo sipping.

 Agedashi tofu

 Grilled lemongrass chicken

 Classic, BYO

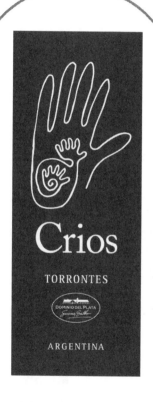

7798068480300

British Columbia

Gehringer Brothers

2013 Private Reserve Riesling
$14.99

Get up, stand up; stand up for your Riesling. Here's a standup Riesling at a button-down price. No need to be concerned about the outlay on this bottle, though you will certainly take notice while sipping on this invigorating white. A bold style overall— bright apple fruit leads off in a quite lean style featuring bracing intensity and a tart, twangy finish.

 On its own

 Chicken salad sandwich

Classic, Romance

623871020009

British Columbia

Mission Hill

2012 5 Vineyards Chardonnay
$14.99

At the end of the day, just let me kick my feet up with a glass of good Chardonnay. This little respite would be better if served up with some conversation, but then again, even a private moment of contemplation to file away the day's wins and tribulations is fine. Pair this glass of MH 5V Chardonnay with a roast chicken, whether home-cooked or store-bought rotisseried, and life would truly be golden. Sourced from vineyard sites throughout the Okanagan, this is simply a solid white. Featuring a great, creamy texture but still balanced and bright, it certainly punches above its price point.

Roast chicken

Tofu scramble

Wednesday Wine,
Winter Warmer

776545985149

 New Zealand

Kono

2013 Sauvignon Blanc
$15.99

New Zealand Sauvignon Blanc is often described as musky. I get the intent; there is certainly an engaging pungency to many a Marlborough Sauvignon Blanc. But my immediate reaction is to think of Kiwi SB as musk, the archetypal old-school masculine perfume. Which is an intriguing idea; the thought of dabbing wine under the armpit has its merits. But ultimately, I prefer to keep my aromas wafting out of the wineglass. Kono's Sauv Blanc is certainly fun to smell: citrus fruit, herbaceous notes, etc. It's a lighter-style Sauvignon Blanc overall, with intense freshness and a very tart finish.

 On its own

 Spaghetti alle Vongole

 Wednesday Wine, Romance

Italy

Ruffino

2013 Lumina Pinot Grigio
$15.99

This is no pushover Pinot Grigio. Pinot Grigio is primo quaffing wine, but the trouble is that, while the bulk of lower-priced Pinot Grigios will ably refresh, they tend not to offer much in the way of character or conversation. Spend a few bucks more and opt for Ruffino's Lumina PG, which provides all the classic citrus, pear skin, and nutty stylings of Italian Grigios while managing to provide something to talk about thanks to enticing floral notes and toothsome texture.

 Tomato bruschetta

 Oyster po' boy

 Wednesday Wine, Rock Out

8001660197156

Spain

Organically Grown

Dominio de Punctum

2012 Viento Aliseo Viognier
$16.50

Biodynamic is like organic taken to the next level. A form of farming developed and championed by Rudolf Steiner in the early 20th century, it takes a huge commitment to follow biodynamic principles. This typically translates into higher price points, but this Bio de La Mancha manages to check in at a very fair $16 and change. Demeter certified (Demeter is the largest certification organization for biodynamic agriculture), this Viognier is soft and approachable, with notes of blossom and stone fruit and just a lick of spice on a dry, balanced finish.

Tamales

Steamed clams

 Wine Geek, BYO

Argentina

Anko

2012 Torrontés
$16.95

This bottle is guaranteed to spark a conversation at your next dinner party. Now, that's not to say that everyone will necessarily be a fan of this wine. Torrontés is just like that thanks to its super-expressive stance, and even for those who don't give in to Torrontés potpourri, they can't help but be intrigued. Anko's bottle hails from the Torrontés high ground of Salta in northern Argentina, and it has all the signatures of the grape: alluring rose-petal and stone-fruit perfume, mouthwatering intensity, and a lingering finish. It's also quite fresh, with a dry citrus kiss to conclude, and makes a great aperitif wine.

 On its own

 Calamari

Patio/Picnic, Wine Geek

859481003082

France

Gabriel Meffre

2012 Saint-Vincent Côtes du Rhône Blanc
$16.99

There's no time like the present to get into some Côtes du Rhône Blanc. Not enough wine drinkers explore these whites, whether out of concern about not knowing the grapes within or simply being lackadaisical about branching out in the wine world. But try it once and I'm pretty confident you'll be back. The back label explains that this elegant white is a blend of mostly Grenache Blanc, Roussane and Clairette Blanche, and it rockets out of the glass with enticing floral and peach aromas in a smooth, honeyed style overall. Show up toting this bottle at your next dinner party and you're sure to impress.

Grilled halibut

 Oysters Rockefeller

 Wine Geek, Rock Out

France

Louis Latour

2012 Ardèche Chardonnay
$16.99

Chardonnay is inspiring. Just ask Big Sean, and perhaps toss on some Marvin Gaye songs. This is to say that Chardonnay is classic. Whether wooing into the night or wishing for memorable conversation, Chardonnay has been through it all and will continue to deliver the wine goods. See for yourself with Louis Latour's classy Ardèche Chardonnay. Hailing from the lesser-known Côteaux de l'Ardèche region in south-central France (holla!), it offers old-school Chardonnay richness and apple nuances in a new-school, vibrant, lemony package.

 Chicken and waffles

Dover sole

 Classic, Romance

3566921000101

British Columbia

Baillie-Grohman

2013 Récolte Blanc
$17.00

This wine is for trailblazers.
Admittedly, the Creston Valley
has yet to become a viticultural
hotbed, but Baillie-Grohman is
working hard to change this.
And with their Récolte Blanc, it's
easy to get behind this boundary-
breaking winery. A blend of
Pinot Gris, Schönburger, and
Kerner sourced from both
Baillie-Grohman's estate
vineyards and sites in Keremeos,
it generously offers aromas of
peach, pear, and flowers. Light
and off-dry in stance, it's all
about bright fruit and easy-
drinking sensibilities.

 On its own

 Spanakopita

 Wine Geek,
Winter Warmer

626990100751

Domäne Wachau

**2012 Terraces Grüner Veltliner
$17.99**

Herein I submit Exhibit A for most sass in a wine bottle. A fantastic, exuberantly fresh Grüner Veltliner hailing from the terrace-lined banks of the Danube River in the Wachau region of Austria, this white certainly brings it—the "it" being citrus and mineral notes in a wine that would merely be posing if its crispness weren't matched to depth and complexity in the form of a little spice, a little honeyed fruit, and a smooth, balanced finish. So not only does it have some cheekiness, it has the great mouthfeel to back it all up.

Thai red curry chicken

Pecorino Pepato

Classic, Patio/Picnic

9007500050987

British Columbia

Gray Monk

2013 Pinot Gris
$17.99

It's no stretch to say that Gray Monk Estate Winery is the godfather of Pinot Gris in B.C. For one, it's the venerable winery's namesake (Pinot Gris is known as Grauer Mönch, or "gray monk," in Austrian). Furthermore, Gray Monk's proprietors played a large role in ushering Pinot Gris into the province, bringing the first Pinot Gris plants from France and encouraging fellow Okanagan grape growers to get on board. More than 40 years later, their Pinot Gris remains a perennial crowd-pleaser. This vibrant white offers gregarious grapefruit and stone-fruit aromas while balancing intensity and freshness with a lick of residual sweetness on the finish.

 On its own

 Scallop ceviche

 Classic, BYO

`778829112203`

Germany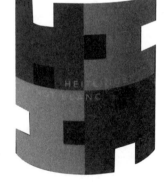

Heitlinger

2011 Smooth Leaf Pinot Blanc
$17.99

In Germany, Pinot Blanc is known as Weissburgunder.
There, it typically produces a dry, fresh, yet mellow style of wine. Baden is a main German wine region for Weissburgunder, and it's home to the Heitlinger "Smooth Leaf" Pinot Blanc. The back label on this bottle explains that the "dew of yellow fruits makes the wine elegant, light and fresh." I'm not entirely sure what that means, but I know that this intense, fruity white with a tangy, slightly bitter finish is a fun take on the Pinot Blanc grape and goes great with grilled salmon.

 On its own

 Grilled salmon

Wine Geek, Patio/Picnic

004040911119

Spain

Ramón Roqueta

2012 Vinya Nostra Xarel-lo
$17.99

Let Xarel-lo be your vinous X factor. If you're looking to take a walk on the wild white wine side, past the Chardonnay and Chenin Blanc, then check out this poignant blanco. A unique grape grown in the Catalonia region of Spain, to date we've typically only found Xarel-lo hiding away as part of the traditional Cava blend triumvirate. But it's also used in still wines, and Vinya Nostra provides an exciting look with its nutty, herby, robust Xarel-lo. There's also great apple and citrus fruit in a wine that is very dry overall and finishes with a deft balance.

Organically Grown

 Chicken Salad

 Sautéed shrimp

 Wine Geek, Rock Out

Yalumba

2013 Y Series Viognier
$17.99

Viognier is seriously engaging. As grapes go, it's about as rich, vibrant, and exotically aromatic as it gets. Originally from France, Viognier has gained fans around the wine world. Yalumba is a pioneer of the grape in Australia, and for years their Y Series Viognier has provided an accessible entry point to this enticing cultivar. What's the fuss? It's vibrant and lush all at once; punchy, yet full of flavour. Chalk it up to sur lie aging, which adds creamy texture and a rich mouthfeel. A solid all-round food wine, it goes well with most weeknight meals.

 On its own

Tandoori fish

 Classic, Winter Warmer

9311789475974

France

Domaine La Rosière

2013 Jongieux
$18.99

Here's one for the serious wine geeks. Actually, this is a sprightly white ready to titillate all wine drinkers. It's not every day you come across a Vin de Savoie, a wine from the Savoy region of France abutting the Alps near Lake Geneva. Here the Jacquère grape reigns supreme in white wines, which in Domaine La Rosière's Jongieux produces an elegant white with great pear-puree and floral nuances, followed by a tart, lengthy finish. It's vibrant yet delicate, the perfect partner for cheese fondue (its customary regional pairing).

 Grilled cheese sandwich (or fondue)

 Shrimp cocktail

 Wine Geek, Romance

626990167167

France

Kuhlmann-Platz

2012 Gewürztraminer
$18.99

Time to represent O.G. Gew.
Old-school Gewürztraminer is
all about Germany and Alsace,
and if you're used to drinking
New World Gewürztraminer,
the Kuhlmann-Platz offers a fun
take on this aromatic grape. On
first sniff, aromas abound: lifted
floral notes, stone fruit, and
super lychee. A soft, fruity entry
marks this as a crowd-pleaser,
with a plush mouthfeel leading
to an off-dry, albeit fresh and
balanced, finish. Overall, it's an
easy-drinking Gewürztraminer
that is great to taste side by side
with a homegrown B.C.
version—in the name of wine
education, of course!

 On its own

 Pho noodle soup

 BYO, Winter Warmer

3306997130704

France

Pfaffenheim

2012 Pfaff Tradition Pinot Gris
$18.99

This is a nice, plush counterpoint to all those prissy, crisp Pinot Grigios. The classic Pfaff Pinot Gris looks serious in the glass from the get-go, all bright golden. Aromas of tropical fruit and citrus lead off in this lush, smooth, and honeyed white that is unabashedly rich. Evident residual sugars await, but this bold white features engaging spice and a smooth finish as counterbalancing flavour measures.

Caramelized onion tart

 Whole-roasted fish

Classic, Romance

3185130071025

Tinhorn Creek

2013 Pinot Gris
$18.99

"Sauerkraut & pork sausage."
This is a food match suggested on the back label of this bottle. It's a curious pick but also informative. It points to the food-pairing prowess of this versatile white, which pours bright light golden in the glass and wafts fruity pear and apple. Good balance overall with a fresh finish, it's just straight-up quality sipping with everything from roast chicken to takeout Thai. Oh, and yes, it also sings right along with the twang of sauerkraut and cuts through rich pork sausage.

Grilled salmon

Grilled sausage

Rock Out, BYO

624802981024

Cono Sur

2013 Single Vineyard Block No. 23 Rulos del Alto Riesling
$19.99

Wineries will go to great lengths to make tasty Riesling. In Cono Sur's case, they headed about as far south as grapes can be grown in Chile to find suitable cool-climate pockets for their Riesling vines: to the Bío-Bío Valley between the Andes and the Coastal Range. So it's only fair that we taste the results of this effort. In fact, their Single Vineyard Riesling is reputedly made from the oldest vines in the Bío-Bío Valley. It shows through great depth and intensity of flavour, with amazing citrus and mineral notes in a bracing white that is both rich yet focused, with deft balance on a lingering, steely finish.

 On its own

 Asiago

 Wine Geek,
Winter Warmer

626990181606

d'Arenberg

2012 The Hermit Crab Viognier Marsanne
$19.99

Stone fruits and spice and everything nice, that's what this tasty white wine is made of! A classic from Australia's coastal McLaren Vale, d'Arenberg's Hermit Crab blends Viognier and Marsanne (two classic white varietals of France's Rhône Valley) to create a sumptuous yet delicate, aromatically charged wine that is simply decadent—in that decadence-that's-good-for-you kind of way. Partial oak-barrel fermentation and maturation adds richness and great texture, and the finish is surprisingly savoury, given the ample fruit upfront. Pair with appetizers or anything harvested from the sea.

Tuna tartare

Seared scallops

Classic, Romance

9311832018004

Kim Crawford

2013 Sauvignon Blanc
$19.99

The hipster wine drinkers may have moved on from New Zealand Sauvignon Blanc. However, there's a good reason why Kiwi Sauv Blanc has achieved mainstream popularity. It's overt and exuberant; in other words, it's the perfect pour for the patio, or anytime a palate pick-me-up is needed really. New Zealand's 2013 vintage has been proclaimed as one for the ages, providing even more motivation for cracking open a bottle of Kim Crawford's latest offering. It oozes textbook tropical-fruit and cut-grass aromas with all the freshness we've come to expect, yet finishes with panache and a lingering sensation that entices the next sip.

 Duck curry

 Lemongrass grilled chops

 Patio/Picnic, BYO

9419227006275

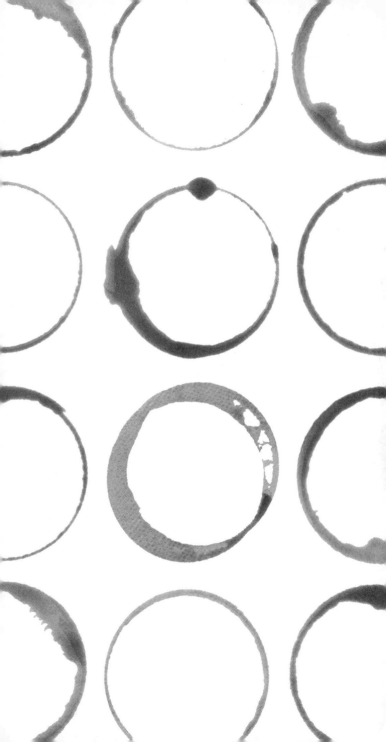

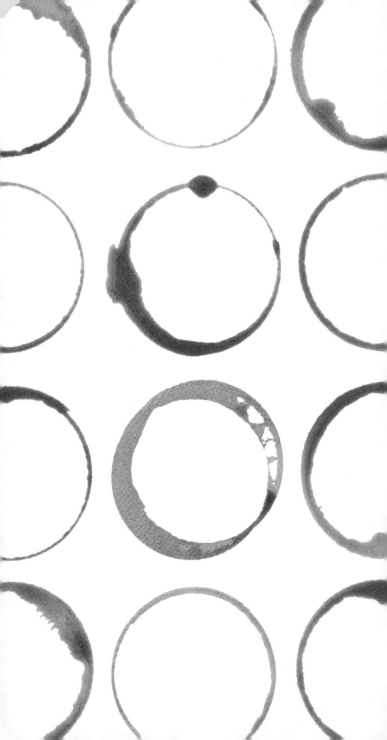

The Pinks

Spain

Olivares

2012 Jumilla Rosado
$12.99

"Let them drink rosé!" This is my favourite refrain when contemplating summertime fêtes. Actually, I'm happy to let my guests drink rosé any time of year. It keeps things easy and works as a fine one-bottle solution: no waffling between white or red, great pairing versatility, etc. At this price, the Olivares Rosado (it's Spanish for rosé) can sate a crowd, and it does so in style. A classic dry pink wine from the Jumilla region in southern Spain, it blends Monastrell (70%) and Syrah (30%) grapes together in a wine that is deep pink with orange highlights featuring berry and earthy notes. It's fresh and fruity with just a lick of spice on its rich finish, and it's good to get the dinner party jumping.

Falafel

Pulled pork

BYO, Classic

Chile

Miguel Torres

Organically
Grown

2013 Las Mulas Cabernet
Sauvignon Rosé
$13.99

**You know when something is
kind of over-the-top but not
quite?** Like a joke that makes
you laugh queasily? Or that
second doughnut? Las Mulas
Rosé is right at that tipping
point. Neon pink in the glass, it
looks like (and nearly tastes like!)
raspberry juice. Following the
theme, it features lots of ripe
berry and an off-dry entry, and a
juicy finish that defines quaf-
fable. The final kicker? It's made
with organically grown grapes.

On its own

Samosas

Patio/Picnic,
Wednesday Wine

8410113002068

British Columbia

Mission Hill

2013 5 Vineyards Rosé
$15.99

Are there any wine truisms? I don't subscribe to many wine rules, but I do believe that pink wine will pair with pretty much anything off the grill. Rosé tends to be both fruity and fresh, traits that work remarkably well with grilled foods. Rosé also tends to bring richness, making it a good match for meatier dishes. In short, it's a barbeque all-rounder, and Mission Hill's latest vintage of 5 Vineyards Rosé highlights this prowess well, thanks to generous berry fruit and a robust, but lip-smacking, fresh finish.

Grilled halibut

Grilled leg roast

Patio/Picnic, Classic

776545995872

British Columbia

Quails' Gate

2013 Rosé
$15.99

Classic picnic pink. Which is to say, this rosé is meant for dining in the great outdoors. Sure, it will taste fine inside as well, but fresh air and a warm breeze really amplify the enjoyment from this vibrant wine's aromas of berries and herbs. Predominantly Gamay Noir (60%), with Pinot Noir (30%) and Pinot Gris (10%) also featured in the mix, it's a solid everyday rosé that pours a nice light pink and finishes fruity and gregarious. So bring on the charcuterie platter and a patio chair.

 Charcuterie

 Chaource

 Romance, BYO

778856112245

Argentina

Marqués de Cáceres

2012 Rioja Rosado
$16.99

Showing up to dinner toting a bottle of Rosado sends a signal that you mean business. Rosé feels like it's coming into vogue as everyone catches on that not all pink wine is sweet and simple, but most people seem to gravitate towards pink wines from France and B.C. Stay ahead of the curve with Spanish Rosado. There's just as much history of pink wine in Spain, which also favours a drier style. Renowned Rioja winery Marqués de Cáceres uses the region's same Tempranillo and Garnacha (Grenache) grapes to craft a coral pink-coloured beauty sporting berry and floral notes. It's very dry throughout and ends with a tart, crisp finish.

 On its own

Turkey burgers

Classic, Wine Geek

8410406611007

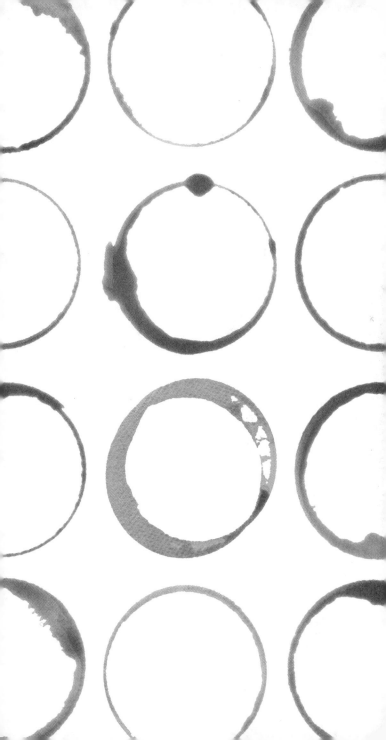

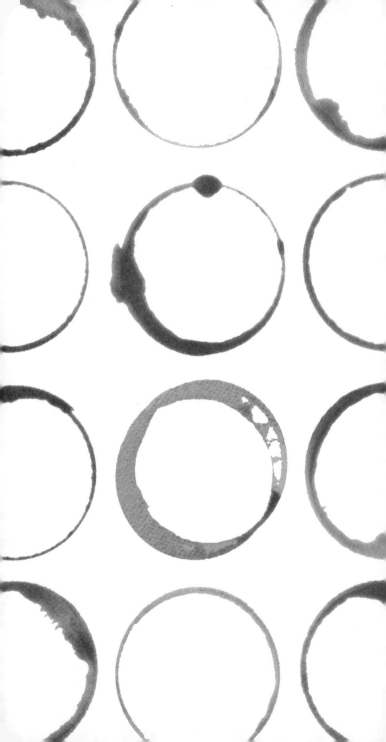

The Reds

Italy

Benvenuto

2012 Barbera
$8.99

No, it's not "that" Barbera. We're talking Barbera of Samnium, the historic region in southern Italy. Not the more famous Barbera of Piedmont, way up in the country's north. While perhaps not as sophisticated as its northern sibling, it's not as though you'll find northern Barbera at under 10 bucks a bottle. So rejoice in this gushy, fresh, strawberry/cotton-candy, fruity red. It's almost spritzy, and downright giddy, in its aim to provide full-on flavour for little investment. Really, what more can we ask for in an everyday barbeque quaffer?

Burgers

Nachos

Wednesday Wine, BYO

8013392000451

Castillo de Monséran

2012 Garnacha
$9.99

Just put it on repeat. Honestly, I'm running out of ways to write up this wine each year because it seems to be a Had a Glass fixture. Think it's best to just rehash what's been said because the wine hasn't really changed. And yes, that is a very good thing for budget-conscious wine enthusiasts. So here goes: Yep, it's still 10 bucks (again). Yup, still a mouthful of juicy berry fruit and smooth, fun, unoaked goodness (again). And yes, it still goes gangbusters with a diverse array of meals, from roast chicken to roast duck (and no doubt roast tofu as well) (again).

Roast chicken

Tex-Mex tofu tacos

Rock Out, Patio/Picnic

831906002788

Chile

Concha y Toro

2013 Frontera Carmenere
$9.99

Carmenere is one grape that should continue to gain attention. The *vinifera* once mistaken for Merlot in Chile, it certainly has its own story to tell, one that fans of rich reds such as Malbec or Mourvèdre should enjoy. Actually, Frontera's fun new label reads as a good abridged story of Carmenere, so it's no stretch to say that you are buying this wine for "educational" purposes. It offers vibrant ripe berry fruit and complementary green-bean undertones, with a fruity and easygoing finish. All told, it's a great introduction to the grape (at a price that shouldn't cause hesitation).

 On its own

Chili

 Wednesday Wine, BYO

626990178873

La Casona de Castaño

2013 Monastrell
$9.99

Thanks to its warm disposition and sun-baked soils, Yecla is magnificent Monastrell territory. Monastrell is a robust grape prone to producing slightly rustic reds (it's known as Mourvèdre in France). It has a long history in Spain, and Bodegas Castaño is a prominent Monastrell champion. But enough talk: for a great introduction to the grape, check out their La Casona de Castaño. At 10 bucks, this sultry Monastrell seriously overdelivers, with a firm overall structure bookended by nice berry fruit and a fresh finish.

 Butifarra with chanterelles

 Roast Cornish hen

Classic, Winter Warmer

Periquita

2011 Original
$9.99

Started from the bottom, now we're here. You know, I used to buy Periquita when I was a university student because it was one of the only wines I could afford. Now, I still buy Periquita because it's a darn fine everyday red that offers a heck of a lot of character for 10 bucks. Credit the trio of grapes working together in this Portuguese mix (Castelão, Trincadeira, and Aragonez), which create a plush yet vibrant overall style that matches up with a myriad of daily plates, from cheese-filled ravioli to meat loaf.

Meat loaf

Ravioli with herbed ricotta

 Classic, Rock Out

5601174204000

Argentina

Diego Murillo

2012 Malbec
$10.99

When in doubt, head south.
Diego Murillo is the value-minded line of wines from Bodega Humberto Canale, an outlier of a winery more than a thousand kilometres south of Argentina's main wine-growing region of Mendoza. We're talking Río Negro Province, located at an amazing 39 degrees south latitude and literally guarding the northern entrance to fabled Patagonia. The region's nooks and valleys offer cooler microclimates, lending this Malbec an easygoing nature highlighted by berry fruit and savoury undertones. It's not overly complicated, but it's smooth, versatile, and very easy to get into.

 Carne asada

 Grilled chops

 Wednesday Wine,
Wine Geek

604984111228

Nuviana

2012 Tempranillo Cabernet
Sauvignon
$10.99

**No fuss, no muss, just a robust
red at a friendly price.** Nuviana
bolts Tempranillo to Cabernet
Sauvignon in a slightly stinky,
eminently enjoyable red that is
juicy up front but a bit grippy to
end. The Cabernet shows
through in slightly funky
green-bean nuances, while the
Tempranillo picks up the pace
with juicy red fruit and a touch
of mocha on the finish. Toss in a
classy label, and you have a
showcase red that slips in at an
everyday price.

 Cocoa-rubbed ribs

 Roast duck

 Wednesday Wine,
Rock Out

South Africa

Nederburg

2012 Winemaster's Reserve
Cabernet Sauvignon
$12.99

Proof that tasty wine does not have to break the bank. There's lots going on for the price of admission here, with rich blackberry and currant fronting a bold and juicy mid-palate. This Cab Sauv is fruit-forward, but it remains structured, which makes for a more serious stance overall. Quite dry to end with a slight tannic grip, it's a solid everyday red that doubles for killer barbeque duty on the weekend.

On its own

Meat loaf

Wednesday Wine, BYO

Montenegro

Plantaže

2010 Vranac
$13.43

Time for a bit of grape trivia to stump your dinner guests. What is the most important grape variety in Montenegro? Why, Vranac, of course, which is both a grape and a brand of wine in this Adriatic Sea–fronting nation. Better yet, after you've quizzed your dining companions, uncork a bottle of Plantaže Vranac for a taste. It has a nice, fruity approach, with crushed flower petal, herbs, and berry. Vibrant overall and very dry to finish, there's also a tart spiciness that makes this wine both engaging and easy-sipping.

 Lamb stew

Stuffed peppers

Wine Geek, Patio/Picnic

8600143001005

Anciano

2005 Gran Reserva Valdepeñas
$13.99

A 10-year-old wine for 14 bucks? Well, sign me up. Aged wine is typically associated with high prices, but Anciano offers up a fun look at a mature wine that's easy on the pocketbook. According to Spanish wine law, bottles labelled Gran Reserva must be aged a minimum of five years before release, and this Gran Reserva Tempranillo from the high plains of Valdepeñas has been aged a full seven years before making its way to store shelves (as proudly exclaimed on the bottle). The languid stint in the cellar shows in this mellow, velvety red bedecked with ripe cherry and sunbaked earth.

Baked ham

Stuffed bell peppers

Classic, BYO

5060108901840

South Africa

Flagstone

2012 Longitude
$13.99

This plush red is like a Snuggie for your taste buds. A blend of Shiraz, Cabernet Sauvignon, and Malbec, Flagstone's Longitude caresses the tongue with rich dark fruit and whiffs of savoury olive and vanilla. It's velvety and warming, with peppery spice building on a balanced finish. It would all be a bit too nap-inducing if this robust red didn't also end with lingering freshness.

 Lamb vindaloo

 Roast beef

 Wednesday Wine, Winter Warmer

5010186018701

Kingston Estate

2010 Petit Verdot
$13.99

If Michael is like Cabernet Sauvignon and Tito is like Merlot, then Jackie Jackson is kind of like the Petit Verdot of the Jacksons. That is to say, neither the most important nor the smoothest of grapes, and kind of relegated to a backseat role in the Bordeaux 5. But given a chance to shine solo, we end up with a bottle like Kingston Estate's varietal Petit Verdot. A bombshell of a number from South Australia, it's dense and grippy, full-bodied and intense. There's lots of ripe, bold fruit, to be sure, but also intriguing are the savoury undercurrents of anise and olive, along with a bit of a potpourri pout of a finish.

 Soy protein smokies

 Carne asada tacos

Wine Geek, Patio/Picnic

9318094006336

Las Hermanas

2012 Monastrell
$13.99

This wine is better the next day.
The thing is, we tend to drink
our wines quite young—particularly reds. Sure, it's true that the
majority of wines do not get
better with age. Still, it can be
surprising how a night hanging
out on the counter can mellow
many an exuberant, juvenile
wine. Take this Las Hermanas
Monastrell, for example. While
it shows fine plum and baked
earth upon opening, it really
manages to marry its fruit, floral
tones, and savoury flavours
together on day two. But wait,
there's more! It also happens to
be produced from organically
grown grapes, and it has that
fun, conversation-starting label.

Organically
Grown

8436005760199

Rosemary and wine–
marinated flat-iron steak

Tapenade

BYOB, Winter Warmer

Italy

Melini

2011 Chianti
$13.99

While it may no longer come wrapped in a wicker-clad fiasco, Melini's Chianti nonetheless keeps the Tuscan spirit alive with its squat, curvy bottle. Regardless of form, Chianti remains one of the wine world's most important (and endearing) wine styles. A classic blend of predominantly Sangiovese complemented by other regional grapes, it offers aromas of cherry and sunbaked earth in a velvety, overall robust wine that finishes balanced and fresh.

 Spaghetti and meatballs

 Kale and mushroom lasagna

 Classic, Patio/Picnic

Italy

Cavit

2010 Alta Luna Phases
$14.95

Here's something different for the lover of rich red wines. Hailing from the rarely seen (in these parts, anyways) Dolomiti IGT region deep in the Dolimites, this mountainous red pours a brilliant dark purple-black in the glass. An exotic mix of Teroldego, Lagrein, and Merlot grapes, it offers ripe plum and vanilla to lead before savoury, earthy notes and a punchy finish seal the vinous deal.

8007890005445

 Grilled boar sausage

Monte delle Dolomiti

 Wine Geek, Rock Out

Monasterio de las Viñas

2006 Reserva Cariñena
$14.99

How do you make a wine bottle stand out amidst a sea of colourful labels? Why, you go all-text, of course—basic black letters on a white background. Something akin to this bottle (which also features frosted glass for that extra old-school touch). It's a classy throwback, and the wine inside doesn't disappoint. A gutsy blend of Garnacha, Tempranillo, and Cariñena, it's smooth with plum and berry fruit, yet a tad rustic and earthy, finishing dry with whiffs of sandalwood and toasty oak thanks to 12 months of barrel aging. It's unique and aged for you, and it's a great option for expanding your wine horizons.

 Aged Manchego

 Toasted red quinoa

 Wine Geek, Wednesday Wine

Argentina

Pascual Toso

2013 Cabernet Sauvignon
$14.99

Though Malbec may continue to steal the spotlight, don't overlook Argentina's other robust reds. Take Cabernet Sauvignon, for example. Pascual Toso's latest is gregarious yet respectful, offering great lifted aromatics of cassis and berry framed by an elegant, lighter mouthfeel overall. An approachable balance and sweet tannins further give this sumptuous red a rich and round disposition, making it ready for all manner of food, from salt-and-peppered, simply prepared steaks to pork roast.

Seared sirloin

Sardo

 Classic, Romance

Italy

Raphael

2012 Rosso Piceno
$14.99

One-up your Chianti-loving friends with Rosso Piceno. East of the rolling hills of Tuscany, towards the swelling surf of the Adriatic Sea, awaits Rosso Piceno DOC, an area within the Le Marche region. Here, as in Tuscany, the Sangiovese grape features in red wines. And also as in Tuscany, the Sangiovese is traditionally blended with other grapes. But Rosso Piceno stakes its own claim on robust Montepulciano. A 50/50 mix of Sangiovese and Montepulciano, Raphael's friendly Rosso Piceno has great black-cherry fruit and herbs, with a rich entry and good intensity overall. It's a perfect pizza and pasta wine.

 Lasagna

 Pepperoni pizza

 Wednesday Wine, Classic

893928002023

South Africa

The Wolftrap

2013 Syrah Mourvèdre Viognier
$14.99

It's always wise to have a camping wine in your repertoire. Something to pull out and pair with dinner cooked on the campfire. A wine like The Wolftrap red, which is a gregarious blend of Syrah and Mourvèdre melded with a splash of 2% Viognier. Fruity, earthy, peppery, herby, and smoky—there's a lot going on here. More impressively, it manages to be both bold and structured—in other words, trim and tasty with a spicy yet elegant finish. Oh, and it's topped with a screw cap, so no need to waste weight on a corkscrew at the campsite.

Cast iron skillet steaks

Duck confit

Patio/Picnic, Romance

Argentina

Urban Uco

2012 Malbec Tempranillo
$14.99

This red is not for sweet-tooth types. Sure, it has lots of fruit and a juicy entry, but it's more brooding than fruit-forward. Come to think of it, while Malbec and Tempranillo don't make for a common wine blend, they both tend to produce savoury, earthy wines. True to form, this 50/50 Malbec–Tempranillo mix melds earthy aromas with tobacco and herbs—quite the feat, considering the wine has only seen three months in oak. A dry finish ends things off in a wine that really does scream to be paired with grilled protein.

 Grilled tenderloin

 Teriyaki ribs

 Wednesday Wine, Patio/Picnic

URBAN UCO
MALBEC–TEMPRANILLO
2012
red wine
vin rouge
14.5% alc./vol. 750ml VALLE DE UCO · MENDOZA
PRODUCT OF ARGENTINA – PRODUIT D'ARGENTINE

7798098894412

France

Bouchard Aîné & Fils

2012 Beaujolais
$15.99

Great taste, less filling. The old saw need not only refer to beer. A lot of wines out there are just too much. So dense you almost have to chew through them, such high alcohol that one glass leaves the taste buds a little woozy. Hence the rising interest in lower-alcohol, less extracted wines. Bottles like Beaujolais, which has traditionally offered lots of flavour without the headache. Bouchard Aîné & Fils's Beaujolais is a great introduction to the Gamay of this French region. It offers the classic berry and bramble in a light-bodied red that finishes fresh and vibrant with earthy spice and floral notes—all at a quite reasonable 12% alcohol level.

Mushroom quiche

 Fried chicken

 Classic, Patio/Picnic

3340180000764

Calliope

2012 Figure 8
$15.99

A number of local wines are now sporting British Columbia's BC VQA seal. This guarantees that 100% of the grapes in the bottle are grown within the province, but it does offer winemakers more flexibility in sourcing grapes across regions. In Calliope's case, their wines may be made from grapes grown across both the Okanagan and Similkameen Valleys, though in this vintage of Figure 8 the grapes come from vineyards in Oliver and Osoyoos. A fruit-forward blend of Merlot (54%), Syrah (34%), and Cabernet Sauvignon (12%), it has lots of rich, dark fruit in a plush overall style with nicely integrated oak and some grip and spice on the finish.

 Smoked pork tenderloin

 Hawkins Cheezies

 Wednesday Wine, Winter Warmer

France

Calvet

2011 Reserve Merlot Cabernet Sauvignon
$15.99

This bottle is Euro prep Bordeaux. I'm always amazed at how Europeans can rock that pop-the-collar, preppie thing without coming across as looking silly. Me in a Lacoste polo? Forget about it. Anyway, Bordeaux (as both wine region and type of wine) can be intimidating, but Calvet's Reserve gives us a glimpse at the joy of Bordeaux at an accessible price and style. On the richer side, it offers smooth, ripe fruit and vanilla before letting toasty oak provide a lingering, mouth-drying finish. All in all, a great intro to the more austere world of red Bordeaux.

 On its own

Barbacoa

 Classic, BYO

3159560510300

Chile

Lomas del Valle

2012 Pinot Noir
$15.99

When it comes to Pinot Noir, cool is—well—cool. Thus, it's not surprising to see Lomas del Valle's tasty estate-bottled Pinot calling the coastal Casablanca Valley home. The cooler-climate pockets of Chile's wine regions have started producing some great Pinot Noirs, and prodigious aromas of juicy raspberry mark this fruit-forward, easy-drinking, and crisp red. A lick of spice on the finish ends the affair, and while this bottle could happily be sipped solo, it marries great with a pot of chili or stew.

 On its own

Stew

 Rock Out, BYO

Argentina

Renacer

2013 Punto Final Malbec
$15.99

The stats all check out.
Vineyards more than 50 years
old, a yield of less than four
tonnes per acre. More impor-
tantly, the taste checks out as
well. Lots of savoury olive and
herbs in this full-bodied red.
There's also dense, dark fruit to
chew on. In short, just a
straight-up, very tasty Malbec
aiming to make friends around
the dinner table. There's lots of
wine here for the price.

 Duck breast

 Liver and onions

 Rock Out, Romance

98709085602

Undurraga

2012 Sibaris Pinot Noir
$15.99

This is the wine for contemporary bon vivants. Sibaris (a.k.a. Sybaris) was the legendary city of the Sybarites, the ancient Greek homestead (now geographically a part of southern Italy) that was reputedly the birthplace for full-on seekers of pleasure and luxury. In other words, ancient bon vivants. Or modern-day foodies, dare I invoke the word. Thus, it's a fitting name for a wine, and this Pinot Noir in particular flies the Sybaritic flag proud. Downright hedonistic with plush, ripe berry fruit fleshed out by a smoky veneer and a spice-laden finish, it's a plump PN ready to sensualize all the senses.

 Braised shank

 Morbier

 Rock Out, Romance

7804315304722

 Argentina

Altos Las Hormigas

2012 Malbec Clásico
$16.99

A perennial good value, Altos Las Hormigas's Classic Malbec hasn't changed much since the last vintage—and that's a good thing. It's still supple and super-smooth, with ripe dark fruit and an underlying savoury, herby stance that is both easy to get into and bold enough to get taste buds standing at attention. In an increasing field of Argentine Malbecs, this Mendoza stalwart continues to stand out.

 Wine-marinated flat-iron steak

 Taleggio

 Wednesday Wine, Patio/Picnic

806145000017

France

Louis Bernard

2012 Côtes du Rhône Villages
$16.99

Côtes du Rhône is on a roll these days. Now, of course there are some exquisite bottles from specific sub-appellations throughout the valley that really shine—from Saint Joseph to Gingondas—but they tend to be priced beyond a normal daily wine budget. Then there are solid examples of regional Côtes du Rhône that will pair up fine with the daily meal. But Côtes du Rhône Villages seems to offer a real sweet spot, with more complexity and flavour intensity. In Louis Bernard's case, a buck extra will get you their Villages, and it provides entree into a bold, ripe-fruited red that also features great herbs, spiciness, and baked earth. Nice balance on a fresh and dry finish seals the deal for this all-round robust red.

 Grano Padano

 Grilled shoulder chops

 BYO, Wednesday Wine

Masi

2011 Possessioni Rosso
$16.99

"The secret of getting things done to act!" So said Dante Alighieri. If it's good enough for Dante, then it's good enough for my glass. This is most certainly a storied wine. Made from Sangiovese and Corvina grapes grown in estates belonging to Dante's descendants, Masi's unflinching Possessioni Rosso envelops ripe, dark fruit, vanilla, and wood spice in an overall grippy, structured style. An air of exoticism arrives thanks to short maturation in seldom-used cherry-wood barrels, creating a conversation starter that backs up the talk with the act of tasting.

 Chorizo and clams

 Bollito misto

 Wine Geek, Winter Warmer

France

Monte del Frá

2012 Bardolino
$16.99

Sometimes you can judge a wine by its label. Featuring a whimsical caricature of a monk taking cover under an umbrella in order to fend off falling grape juice (while still attempting to fill his glass, mind you), this bodacious Bardolino has an easygoing, super-fresh, and über-fun style. An invigorating mix of Corvina, Rondinella, and Sangiovese grapes (classic red grapes used in the Bardolino region of northeastern Italy) harvested from 55-year-old vines, the wine showcases a bright ruby colour and tart raspberry fruit and pairs up well with pizza—or anything tomato sauce–based.

 Ham-and-pineapple pizza

 Pasta puttanesca (with anchovies or without)

 Wine Geek, Patio/Picnic

838547000180

Spain

Rio Madre

2011 Rioja Graciano
$16.99

Rioja is the heartland of Spanish wine; it's the region with a well-earned reputation around the world. And while there is no shortage of tasty wines from Rioja, the Rio Madre manages to stand out. Tempranillo is the typical cultivar of Rioja; however, Rio Madre is comprised of 100% Graciano, a grape that usually plays a supportive, blending role to Tempranillo's star turn. Here, Graciano shines in all its dark garnet–coloured glory. It's bold, it's juicy, and it's smooth right through its fruity finish.

 Turkey kebabs

Grilled eggplant

 Wine Geek, Winter Warmer

Australia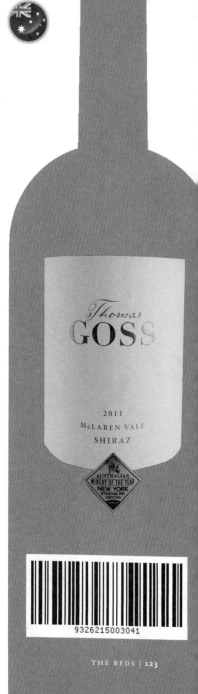

Thomas Goss

2011 McLaren Vale Shiraz
$16.99

This is no paunchy Shiraz. Put away any preconceived notions of Aussie Shiraz lacking deft footwork; Thomas Goss offers it all: the rich, powerful fruit we've come to expect and love from South Australian Shiraz, married to a lively structure featuring lifted floral aromas. Credit the cooling influence of coastal McLaren Vale vineyards, not to mention the winemaking of Ben Riggs. All in all, it's a bold bottle that manages to be both crowd-pleasing and elegant—no easy feat!

 Lamb palak

Aged cheddar

Classic, BYO

9326215003041

U.S.A.

Charles & Charles

2012 Post No. 35 Cabernet
Sauvignon Syrah
$17.99

The first thing you notice is the label. It certainly has a brash, rockstar look. Next, you (literally) pick up on the bottle's heft. Thing is heavy, serious paperweight territory. Which leads to opening, pouring, and first sip. The wine tastes like it looks and feels, which is to say that this is a seriously bold, in-your-face red. An aggressive, engaging mix of ripe berry and savoury notes, including leather and spice, are in full effect, leading to a gritty yet elegant finish that screams power chord (and powerful pour).

 On its own

 Souvlaki

 Rock Out, Winter Warmer

856622001112

La Posta

2013 Tinto Red Blend
$17.99

Straight out of La Boca! La Boca is a famed neighbourhood in Buenos Aires, Argentina's magical capital city. It's described as the birthplace of the tango (not to mention the home of the Boca Juniors football club!), and considered a must-visit for tourists. Looking at a bottle of La Posta evokes the artistry and grandeur of La Boca, and this Malbec–Bonarda–Syrah blend certainly captures the colourfulness of the area. Earthy and robust, leathery yet juicy, it's balanced—but just barely, pushing at the seams to envelop and embrace. Cue the Carlos Gardel and pour a glass.

Grilled rib eye

Merguez sausages

Rock Out, Romance

835603001396

 United States

Renwood

2011 Zinfandel
$17.99

Contemporary Zinfandel walks a fine line. Sure, we want that voluptuous, fruity Zinfandel spirit. But in a rush to be crowd-friendly, these days a lot of Zinfandel appears overripe, overtly fruity, and plain flabby. So it was a pleasant surprise to come across Renwood's entry-level Zin, which is silky-smooth and chock-a-block with berry compote and amped up on all the cinnamon and clove one could want. However, it avoids being obtuse thanks to a solid mid-palate structure and decent freshness, which seriously motivates the next sip.

 Chili

Rice pilaf

Classic, Winter Warmer

Argentina

Trapiche

2012 Pure Malbec
$17.99

It's like bizarro Malbec. Well, not quite, but admittedly, Trapiche's Pure flips the script by delivering a 100% Malbec completely free from oak aging. That's right: unoaked in all its fruity glory! This is certainly a break from the norm, as Malbec and vanilla and toasty oak seem to go hand in hand, but it turns out that the norm tastes just fine with a little refreshing. Lots of savoury qualities like herb and olive lead to a plush and dark fruit core. Quite concentrated overall, it's rich and fruit-forward, but even with all the extroverted fruit, it remains bold and structured.

 On its own

 Burgers

 Romance, Patio/Picnic

7790240094442

Australia

Xanadu

2010 Next of Kin Cabernet Sauvignon
$17.99

Here's a Cabernet Sauvignon with great focus and structure. It's like the "slim cut" version of the wine versus the unfortunately often baggy and boxy stylings of Cab Sauv. But then, this is not surprising, given this bottle hails from the cooler-climate pocket of Margaret River in Western Australia. Margaret River fruit tends toward a leaner, brighter style in general. Lush aromas of black currant and eucalyptus give way to an almost juicy, albeit focused and intense mid-palate. Dry to end, the finish is further bolstered by toasty oak and light tannins.

Kebabs

Braised short ribs

Romance, BYO

9336957000345

British Columbia

Perseus

2012 Cabernet Shiraz
$19.90

This wine strikes a nice balance.
Not quite boisterous, but
certainly not introverted, with
good balance overall for a B.C.
red. An exuberant blend of 48%
Shiraz, 42% Cabernet Sauvignon,
and 10% Cabernet Franc (and
yes, technically that makes the
wine a Shiraz Cabernet), it is
quite fruit-forward with plush
berry fruit and a vanilla-mocha
kiss. Yet it builds to a nice spicy
finish and maintains great
overall poise. In short, a solid
local option to please a crowd.

 On its own

 Reuben sandwiches

BYO, Winter Warmer

626990129653

Argentina

Amalaya

2012 Malbec Blend
$19.99

Smooth operator. It's another vintage and another bold and rich offering from Amalaya, a mostly Malbec blend produced from grapes grown at high elevation in the upper reaches of the Calchaqui Valley in northern Argentina. Expect a nice, complex nose of dark fruit, herbs, and toasty oak followed by a juicy, plush feel in the mouth and an elegant, balanced finish that maintains enough acidity to keep things surprisingly lively for such a rich red.

 On its own

 Rouladen

 Classic, Romance

7798104763022

France

Château Pesquié

2012 Terrasses
$19.99

Ventoux is about as far south as the Rhône Valley gets, just a holler and a mountain range away from Provence. Which means we're reaching serious sunshine and thermal units. In the wrong hands, this combination can lead to overripe, flabby reds. But when done right, as with Ch. Pesquié's latest vintage, Terrasses, the climate creates silky, rich wines. In fact, Terrasses derives from "lump of earth," and you can almost taste the sun-drenched, terrace-lined vineyards. Mostly Grenache and Syrah, there's great dark fruit combined with lifted aromatics in a bold bottle that still manages to finish balanced and fresh.

 Country terrine

 Banon

 Wednesday Wine, Rock Out

Terrasses

VENTOUX – RHÔNE VALLEY VINEYARDS
2012

CHÂTEAU
PESQUIÉ

626990005377

Portugal

Crasto

2012 Douro
$19.99

Let's hear it for sinewy and powerful reds. Proof that big-time flavour doesn't have to carry excess palate-draining baggage, Crasto's latest vintage Douro offers robust dark fruit complemented by amazing lifted perfume and floral tones. It's certainly dense and chewy, but this bold blend of four of Portugal's most common red grapes (Tinta Roriz, Tinta Barroca, Touriga Franca, and Touriga Nacional) maintains great focus and balance. The result is a big but fresh wine, one that is surprisingly lip-smacking for being so intense.

 Chanfana

 Pico

 Classic, Winter Warmer

France

Maison des Bulliats

2012 Régnié
$19.99

I'm happy that the wines of Beaujolais appear to be gaining more fans. But I'm also concerned. Concerned that it's costing me more to enjoy good Beaujolais in general, and specifically concerned that this Cru Beaujolais may price itself right out of *Had a Glass*. The cost of bottles of Beaujolais is up across the board, with Maison des Bulliats's Régnié a hefty two bucks more than last year. But you know, it's still the best Cru for the money, still full of the tasty essence of the Gamay grape (that beguiling combination of fruit and bramble, perfume and earth), and still wonderfully intense for such a light and vibrant red wine.

Burgers

Eggplant confit

Classic, Rock Out

 Italy

Tenuta Cocci Grifoni

2008 Le Torri Rosso Piceno Superiore
$19.99

There's an Italian word, sprezzatura, that captures this wine well. Loosely, it refers to a "studied carelessness or nonchalance." Essentially, looking good without looking like you tried to look good. Le Torri is sprezzatura in a bottle. A Rosso Piceno Superiore, it's a blend of Montepulciano and Sangiovese grapes that spends 14 months aging in Slovenian oak barrels. It effortlessly envelops the mouth with sumptuous dark fruit, then seamlessly builds to a strong, grippy finish with firm overall structure. In short, it manages to be a big, bold red without resorting to overt, overripe gestures.

Bresaola

White-truffle risotto

Wine Geek, Rock Out

Italy

Tommasi

2012 Le Prunée Merlot
$19.99

This is what happens when Merlot goes on the Paleo diet. Wait a minute, that doesn't work because wine is not considered Paleo-proper. All right, maybe it's more of a Zone diet? The point is, at 12.5% alcohol and expressing elegance, this is a trimmed-down, vibrant red. Which doesn't mean it's stripped of flavour. Quite the contrary, it shows lots of plum and floral aromas, not to mention it's plush and finishes with great balance. All in all, a nice counterpoint to the notion that Merlot is soft and boring, and proof that strength and heft can coexist with structure.

 Porchetta roast

 Duck breast

Patio/Picnic, BYO

8004645366103

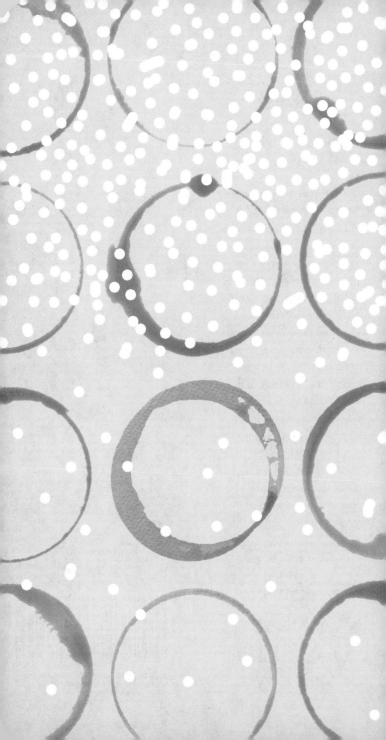

The Sparkling

Germany

Black Tower

2012 Pink Bubbly
$12.99

"Wine doesn't have to be complicated to be good." This was the majority comment heard around the table while tasting Black Tower's new Pink Bubbly. It's true. While this bottle is not going to take home the prize for most sophisticated pink, it certainly wins an award for most fun. I can't even tell you what grapes are in the bottle, as Black Tower explains it's a "cuvée" of grapes grown in the "European Community." Not exactly a full-on fizz, it's semi-sparkling and pours a frothy light pink. It's sweet, to be sure, but more memorably, it's full of red fruit and finishes fresh with a light touch—providing more than enough motivation for the next (large) sip.

Whitefish curry

Jerk chicken

Rock Out, Patio/Picnic

4069600014424

South Africa

Meander

Moscato
$13.99

Dessert in a glass. It's as simple as that. Sure, you could cut up some fresh fruit to get fancy; you can even serve it aside a slice of cake. Heck, if you have more of a savoury tooth, you could even break out the grilled oysters or salty blue cheese. Whichever way your end-of-the-meal leans, this bottle of Meander Moscato is ready to leisurely, umm, meander there with you. This super-expressive Muscat of Alexandria offers lots of peach and orange-blossom notes in a sweet bottle of fizz that finishes fresh enough. It's fun and fizzy, and sometimes that's all we need!

On its own

Fruit salad

Romance, BYO

6009814420558

Organically
Grown

 Italy

Anna Spinato

Prosecco Brut Organic
$14.95

Fun packaging? Check. Popular Prosecco inside the bottle? Check. Organically grown grapes? Check. Good value? Check. Anna Spinato's Prosecco Organic is right on trend, and really, there's not much to argue about with this fun and lively, fruity and fresh sparkling wine. Aromas of fruit and flowers abound, and though there's honeyed notes and a hint of sweetness, this Brut Prosecco finishes crisp. With a delicate and lighter style overall, this bubbly is great simply sipped solo or served with egg-based dishes.

On its own

Eggs Benny

 Romance, BYO

8011204003874

Italy

Riondo

Prosecco
$14.99

Heads up: you'll need a corkscrew to get into this bottle of bubbly. Fortunately, that's the most difficult aspect of enjoying this outgoing Prosecco. The bottle topper recommends a butterfly-type opener, but I managed just fine with a trusty old waiter's friend. Once the cork has been cocked, the wine exposed proves to be fresh and fruity with a light touch and a Pez-candy finish—well worth the effort, not to mention a great fizz for cutting through rich sauces or fatty foods.

Salmon burgers

Pasta alfredo

Wednesday Wine, Rock Out

010086100471

Italy

Casolari

Lambrusco di Sorbara
$15.99

Everyone should have a go-to sparkling red in their wine repertoire. Red bubbles tend to make for killer BBQ wines, can be hugely refreshing when served cold right out of the fridge, and offer a different spin on the wine norm. Sparkling reds come in all types, from fresh to heavy, dry to sweet. Casolari's Lambrusco di Sorbara hits the right balance for most occasions. It pours a captivating ruby in the glass and is light and frothy. There's a fun mix of tart berry fruit and earthy notes, good acidity, and just enough residual sugars to end things smooth and easy. All said, it leaves the palate feeling fresh—more lip-smacking than tongue-coating.

LAMBRUSCO
DI SORBARA
DENOMINAZIONE DI
ORIGINE PROTETTA

CASOLARI

On its own

Smokies or sausages

 Patio/Picnic, BYO

8032150001011

Terra Andina

Sparkling Moscato
$15.99

Sparkling wine from Brazil? Say what?! In fact, not only is bubbly widely enjoyed in Brazil, but much of it is produced in this South American country. It's just that we don't get to see much of it. Terra Andina's Sparkling Moscato is the first Brazilian wine widely available locally, and it resounds with tropical fruit and an orchard's worth of orange aromatics. The bottle says this wine is "Free-spirited by nature," and indeed this crowd-pleasing, sweeter-style fizz is ready to serve all year long. It's not quite lounging on Copacabana, but it's a lot less expensive than a plane ticket!

 On its own

 Shrimp pastel

 Wine Geek, Patio/Picnic

Germany

Henkell

Riesling Dry
$16.99

What's in a package? The classy black-and-gold label screams sophistication, and the easy-going, fruity style will leave them reaching for a refill. Henkell's non-vintage Riesling sparkler oozes apple and peach in a very approachable manner that finishes slightly sweet. Pour with the canapé cart, or use as a base for mimosa cocktails.

4003310010871

Mimosa cocktail

Fried coconut shrimp

Winter Warmer, BYO

Segura Viudas

Brut Reserva Cava
$16.99

The bottle may have an updated look, but the bubbly inside remains tasty and classic. Always an easy go-to Cava pick, Segura Viudas's Brut Reserva just works. A slightly off-dry, fruity entry builds into a rich, intense sparkling wine redolent with apple and lemon. Its fresh, robust finish still features some roughness—it's never been the smoothest of sparklers—but that is what adds to its character.

Pigs in blankets

Kale and quinoa salad

Classic, Romance

33293690009

 Italy

Vaporetto

Prosecco
$17.99

A *vaporetto* is a public water bus or ferry that cruises the canals of Venice. Prosecco is the sparkling wine of record in the Veneto region of northeastern Italy. Venice, considered one of the world's most romantic cities, is the capital and largest city of Veneto. You get the theme. And while it would certainly be romantic to sip on a glass of Prosecco while crisscrossing Venice's canals, in the meantime you can create an homage at home by picking up a bottle of Vaporetto, hopping on the Aquabus to Granville Island, and grabbing market ingredients for a meal. Heady bubbles, lots of citrus and floral notes, good intensity, and a dry finish buoy this bubbly.

On its own

Pasta primavera

 Romance, Patio/Picnic

8000872071018

Italy

Belstar

Cuvée Rosé Extra Dry
$18.99

Sparkling rosé is not a top-of-mind pick for most people. But it should be! It's fun, it's rich, and it tends to pair amazingly well with a huge array of food, from grilled anything to takeout dynamite rolls. Belstar's Cuvée Rosé is full of ripe berry fruit with a rich mouthfeel and a lush but crisp finish. The cool, art deco–inspired label says "Extra Dry," but remember: for sparkling wine, that still means evident residual sugar (or sweetness), which ramps up the quaffing factor. Serve well chilled to maximize good times.

 Grilled ling-cod tacos

Grilled rib eye

Rock Out, Winter Warmer

8000872049017

California

Organically
Grown

Parés Baltà

Brut Cava
$19.99

This Brut Cava pours a delightful straw colour with subtle green tinges. Pear and apple aromas waft from this sprightly Spanish sparkler, which is made from the three classic Cava grapes (Parellada, Macabeo, and Xarel-lo) that are organically grown in the Penedès region near Barcelona. Fantastically fresh and crisply acidic, this lighter-bodied sparkling wine is perfect paired with crab cakes or fried chicken, or simply an empty seat on a patio.

 On its own

 Crab cakes

Patio/Picnic, BYO

8410439034354

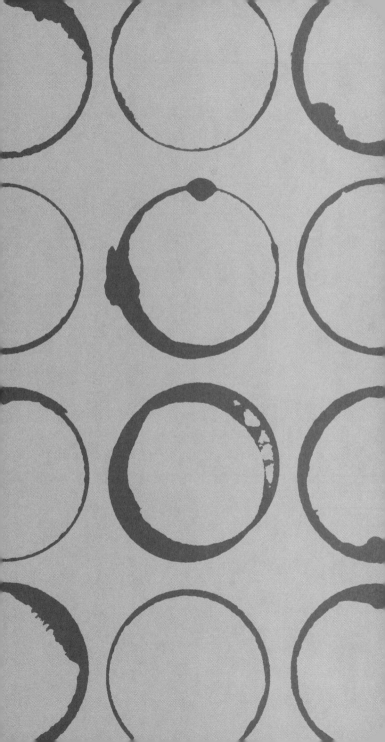

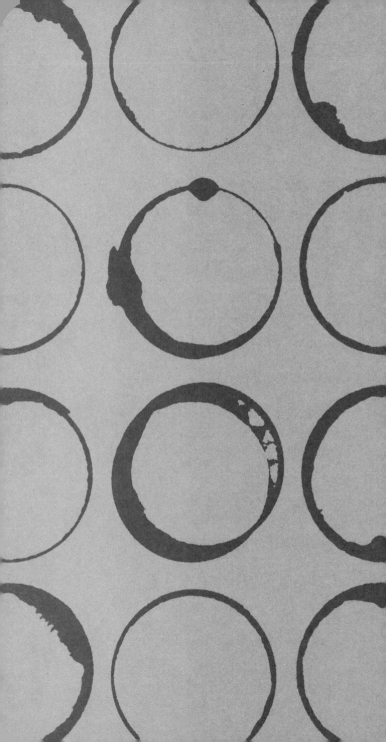

The Fortifieds

Emu

Australian Apera Medium Dry
$11.59

"Australian Apera" has a nice ring to it. It's certainly better than the Amontillado Medium Dry Sherry tag the bottle used to wear. The thing is, sherry is really only sherry when produced in the Jerez region of Spain. But notable fortified wines are made around the world, and, after signing an agreement with the European Commission to stop using the term "sherry," Australia came up with the name Apera. So for a good introduction to the "medium dry" style of fortified wines, check out this dark-golden, amber nectar. There's lots of citrus and apple to lift this nutty, raisiny, rich wine that, sipped chilled (or even on the rocks), serves as either a great start or end to a meal.

 On its own

 Salted mixed nuts

 Wednesday Wine, BYO

Portugal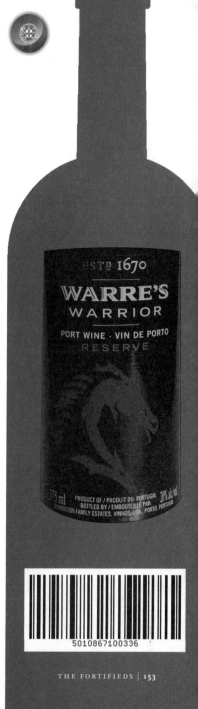

Warre's

Warrior Reserve Port
$13.49 for 375mL

Unfortunately, there's a dearth of value-priced ports available locally. Fortunately, Warre's Warrior Reserve Port remains on shelves and is one fantastic option. So it's back in *Had a Glass* to fulfill an important role in every wine fan's repertoire. For wine doesn't just end at the whites and reds (or perhaps the pinks and sparkling). No, it's important to flip to the end of the book (or the end of the meal, as it were) and remember the fortified wines! Despite its combative name, this port is actually rather easygoing, full of rich dark fruit, some baking spices, and a sumptuous mouthfeel that makes a fine tipple to end the evening.

 Goat brie

 Dark chocolate mousse

 Wine Geek, Romance

Portugal

Taylor Fladgate

2009 Late Bottled Vintage Port
$15.99 for 375mL

Late Bottled Vintage Port is the blue-collar Vintage Port. Not only is Vintage Port rather expensive, it requires serious time in the cellar before it approaches optimum drinkability. So, sure, we'd all love to sip on well-loved, well-aged Vintage Port, but short of having a generous trust fund or possessing some serious foresight, for the time being the hoi polloi will be sipping Late Bottled Vintage. As well-regarded independent port house Taylor Fladgate explains, LBV is still lovingly "blended from selected wines of a single harvest." It's also still redolent with enough sumptuous, yet structured, plum and caramel tones to make us feel like a million bucks.

 On its own

 Dark chocolate chunks

 Classic, BYO

Alvear

Amontillado
$17.99

Here's a sweet wine for non-fans of sweet wine. Honestly. While this Spanish fortified certainly comes across rich and sweet, it is anything but cloying. If your sherry reference point revolves around "cream," then it's time to expand your sherry horizons. This is a great introduction to the unique Amontillado style, which is essentially a fino sherry minus its protective cap of flor that undergoes a slow, flavour-enhancing oxidation. It pours a rich bronze in the glass, and on first sip it coats the mouth with savoury, classic, nutty, and dried-fruit flavours. The finish is bold but deft, with no syrupy heaviness, making this an amenable fortified. Serve cold from the fridge.

 On its own

 Bleu de Bresse

 Rock Out, Classic

Spain

González Byass

Nutty Solera Medium Sherry
$17.99

Nutty Solera is like the awl on a Swiss Army knife. Seldom employed, but it's actually a pretty useful little tool. You can use it to punch a new hole in a belt or stitch up a pair of leather chaps. In desperate times, it even serves as a corkscrew of last resort. Nutty Solera is an Oloroso, or "scented," sherry, imbued with the great amber colour and nutty nuances from its unique oxidative winemaking process. It's a darn fine pre- or post-dinner tipple, particularly with nuts and/or a cheese plate. Best of all, it comes topped with a reusable cork plug—no corkscrew required!

 Peanut brittle

 Gruyère

 Wine Geek, Wednesday Wine

Italy

Florio

2010 Vecchioflorio Marsala
Superiore Dolce
$18.99

**Sure, Marsala is great for
cooking, but it makes for fine
sipping, too.** It's time to switch
up your fortified wine routine!
Like Port, this storied fortified
from the Italian isle of Sicily has
varying designations, with
Marsala Superiore indicating that
the wine is aged at least two years.
A gorgeous amber colour, it's rich
and ripe and oozes raisin and
dates, vanilla and caramel. It's a
fine after-dinner treat that
seriously warms the cockles.

On its own

Toasted almonds

Romance, Winter Warmer

891006001012

France

Lillet

Blanc
$18.99

Lillet continues its Had a Glass run. For good reason. It is a versatile, verifiable classic bottle steeped in aperitif-ian history. Of course, this aromatic fortified wine from France also happens to be steeped in a secret blend of macerated liqueurs created mostly from a bevy of citrus peels, which is the key to Lillet's lip-smacking prowess. Melding a balance of bitter and sweet, it is perfect for solo sipping with a slice of orange or lemon during the approach to dinner, but also deftly adds a layer of flavour in famous cocktails like the Vesper and Corpse Reviver #2. And remember, with only an ounce used here and there, a bottle of Lillet tends to go a long way.

 On its own

 Root veg chips

 BYO, Wednesday Wine

The Cocktails

White
DIY Wine Cooler

Remember in the '80s when wine coolers were all the rage? As a child of the '80s, it's not like I even touched a drop of alcohol. Yet I clearly recall being enamoured by those two old dudes on television hocking Bartles and Jaymes "Premium" Wine Coolers. Truly, chilling on a porch with a wine cooler sounds like a great idea regardless of the year, though coolers don't seem all that cool these days. But if '80s music and fashion can come back, there's no reason '80s wine coolers can't get back into glasses. There's also no reason for buying sugary, pre-made wine coolers when crafting your own DIY version is so simple and rewarding.

Makes 1 wine cooler

4 oz	fruity, unoaked white wine (a Pinot Grigio or Sauvignon Blanc, for example pages 63 and 48, would put the cool in wine cooler!)
6 oz	lemon-lime soda (or go fancy with artisanal pop, as you prefer)
2 oz	fresh citrus juice (I favour lemon, lime, orange, or pineapple)
	fruit slices, to garnish

Combine wine, soda, and fruit juice over ice in a tumbler or any porch-worthy drinking vessel. Add fruit to garnish, insert straw or swizzle stick, and enjoy.

Pink

The Rosé Gin and Tonic (RG&T)

Necessity, it's often said, is the mother of invention. The RG&T arose out of a need to take the gin and tonic to another level. Actually, it's a twist on the classic Pink Gin and Tonic, which itself was a necessary invention to tame the fires of very classic Pink Gin. Pink Gin is simply gin spiked with a few healthy dashes of Angostura Bitters, which lends the drink a pretty pink colour and a curious depth of bitterness and complexity. Of course, this tastes as strong as it sounds, so the Pink Gin and Tonic adds tonic water and a lemon wedge to create a more affable high ball. Swap the bitters for rosé, add pomegranate juice, and you arrive at the RG&T, which has quickly become a necessary backyard lounging accessory.

Makes 1 cocktail

2 oz	gin, preferably Plymouth
1 oz	pomegranate juice
1 oz	rosé wine (for example, page 84)
1 oz	tonic water
	lemon slice

Fill a tall glass with ice and pour in gin, pomegranate juice, and rosé. Stir to mix, then top with tonic water and garnish with a slice of lemon.

Red
The Hot Frenchman

Yes, essentially this is a single serving-sized take on mulled wine. But, boy, doesn't Hot Frenchman sound more exciting than "Hot Red Wine!" Anyways, at least the name gives pause and something to mull over, because the preparation is pretty darn simple. The thing is, while a pot of hot wine is great for hosting gatherings, it's overkill when you're sitting solo on a cold winter's night and one mug will do. For authenticity's sake, use a bottle of Bordeaux, or "Claret" as the Brits used to say, but truth be told turning up the heat on any rich red will create a fine Hot Frenchman.

Makes 1 mug

4 oz	rich red wine (for example, page 119)
1 oz	orange liqueur such as Grand Marnier
1/2	tsp sugar
1/2	oz fresh squeezed orange juice
1/2	oz fresh squeezed lemon juice

Gently warm red wine in a non-reactive pot or saucepan (you want the wine to get hot, but please do not let it come to a boil). Dissolve sugar in wine, then add orange liqueur and fresh juices. When wine has reached desired heat level, pour into a heat-resistant toddy glass or coffee mug and settle in.

Sparkling
The Mimosa

Simple and time-tested, the Mimosa will forever remain a classic sparkling wine cocktail. Sure I love my Champagne cocktails and my French 75s, but for ease of preparation, daytime versatility, and darn good taste—it's tough to beat the Mimosa*. Plus, the Mimosa was my grandpa's go-to weekend brunch libation, so it always arrives with a whiff of pleasant nostalgia and reflection. Now Gramps was fond of mixing Minute Maid and cheap California Brut, but I do find it's worth the little added fore-thought and effort required for freshly squeezed juice. Similarly, the proportions are debatable depending on your preference— but the following serves as a good starting point.

Makes 1 glass

3 oz	fresh squeezed orange juice
3 oz	quality sparkling wine (for example, page 141)

Pour orange juice into a Champagne flute. Top with sparkling wine.

*If the Mimosa seems a tad too pedestrian for your tastes, you can always adjust the ratio of OJ to sparkling wine upwards to 3-to-1 and add a splash of grenadine. Now you have a Buck's Fizz, which certainly sounds more intriguing and, apparently, is a London-originating recipe that actually predates the Mimosa!

Fortified
Sherry Cobbler

Sherry makes a magnificent cocktail ingredient. You wouldn't necessarily think this from the generally lacklustre appreciation still plaguing sherry these days, however it has a lengthy history in cocktail culture, particularly in the American South, where sherry and other fortified wines were once a mainstay. From dry sherry to sweet cream sherry, these fine fortified wines have a hand in many classic cocktails and are also being used more and more by in-the-know bartenders looking to create modern tipples with a twist. On the classic side of the spectrum, consider the Sherry Cobbler. It is a quintessential American classic (though it truly is such an adaptable cocktail that it can be construed in so many postmodern ways).

Makes 1 cocktail

4 oz	Fino or Amontillado sherry (see page 155 for inspiration)
1 1/2 tsp	superfine sugar
1	orange slice
3–4	berries (though any fruit on hand will suffice)
1	straw (the Sherry Cobbler is reputed to have popularized the straw)

Cut the orange slice in half and stuff into a mixing glass or cocktail shaker. Fill with ice, pour in sherry, add sugar, and proceed to shake vigorously while reciting your ABCs (or at least until the sugar is dissolved). Pour into a tall Collins glass filled with fresh crushed ice, and garnish with seasonal berries. For maximum refreshment (and ease), drink through a straw.

Index by Country

Château Pesquié Terrasses 131
Domaine La Rosière Jongieux 74
Gabriel Meffre Saint-Vincent
   Côtes du Rhône Blanc 66
Lillet Blanc 158
Louis Bernard Côtes du Rhône
   Villages 119
Louis Latour Ardèche
   Chardonnay 67
Maison des Bulliats Régnié 133
Kuhlmann-Platz Gewürztraminer
   75
Paul Mas Viognier 58
Pfaffenheim Pfaff Tradition Pinot
   Gris 76
La Vieille Ferme Blanc 54

Germany
Black Tower Pink Bubbly 138
Heitlinger Smooth Leaf Pinot
   Blanc 71
Henkell Riesling Dry 144

Hungary
Dunavar Muscat Ottonel 50

Italy
Anna Spinato Prosecco Brut
   Organic 140
Belstar Cuvée Rosé Extra Dry 147
Benvenuto Barbera 92
Casolari Lambrusco di Sorbara 142
Cavit Alta Luna Phases 106
Ciao Sangiovese 27
Florio Vecchioflorio Marsala
   Superiore Dolce 157
Masi Modello Bianco 55
Masi Possessioni Rosso 120
Melini Chianti 105
Monte del Frá Bardolino 121

Raphael Rosso Piceno 109
Riondo Prosecco 141
Ruffino Lumina Pinot Grigio 63
Ruffino Orvieto Classico 56
Tenuta Cocci Grifoni Le Torri
   Rosso Piceno Superiore 134
Tommasi Le Prunée Merlot 135
Vaporetto Prosecco 146

Montenegro
Plantaže Vranac 100

New Zealand
Kim Crawford Sauvignon Blanc
   80
Kono Sauvignon Blanc 62

Portugal
Crasto Douro 132
Gazela Vinho Verde 51
Periquita Original 96
Taylor Fladgate Late Bottled
   Vintage Port 154
Warre's Warrior Reserve Port 153

South Africa
Flagstone Longitude 102
Meander Moscato 139
Nederburg Winemaker's Reserve
   Cabernet Sauvignon 99
Obikwa Sauvignon Blanc 48
The Wild Olive Old Vines Chenin
   Blanc 57
The Wolftrap Syrah Mourvèdre
   Viognier 110

Spain
Alvear Amontillado 155
Anciano Gran Reserva Valdepeñas
   101

United States

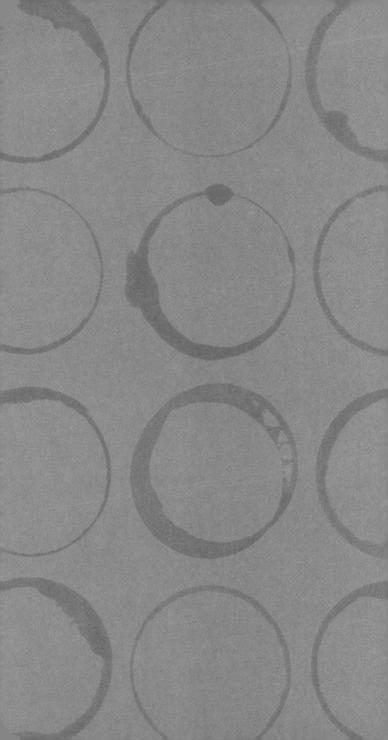

Index by Type

Acknowledgements

As always, *Had a Glass* relies upon an utterly amazing cast of talented, creative, and supportive people to keep my wineglass swirling. You readers, first and foremost, are the inspiration for all the sipping and tasting..

Thanks again to Robert, Zoë, Trish, Lindsay, and the entire Appetite and Penguin Random House Canada teams for giving me the opportunity to bring *Had a Glass* to life. Thanks too to all the grape growers, winemakers, wineries, agents, and wine shops going out of their way to ensure new wines find their way to our glasses. I also want to acknowledge the venues that have long given me space and column inches to spread the wine love, in particular *The Province* newspaper and TASTE magazine. And a shout-out once again to Le Marché St. George, the best little neighbourhood grocer that is nothing short of an oasis in East Van.

Respect is due to Kenji, my original partner in wine crime and the co-creator of *Had a Glass*. You are missed in geography but never feel far away. *Had a Glass* will always remain as much a legacy of your creative energies.

Finally, thank you to my family and friends. The former has cellar-worthy patience, the latter cellar-worthy thirst, and together you provide an amazing support network that makes this book possible.

About the Author

JAMES NEVISON is an award-winning wine writer, educator, and the co-founder of HALFAGLASS wine consultancy in Vancouver. James has co-authored eight bestselling wine books, and he is widely known as "The Wine Guy" from his weekly column in *The Province* newspaper. James also contributes regularly to TASTE magazine, and his casual and accessible take on wine is often heard and seen on radio and television. James has judged wine competitions in Canada and internationally, and in 2009 he was honoured to be named one of *Western Living* magazine's "Top 40 Foodies Under 40."